What Readers Are Saying

"Can a book heal? This one does. It has an energy that is released to the reader. I felt it. As a healer myself, I could relate to everything Diane so candidly describes. If you read only one book on healing make it this one. This book should be a movie."

— Susan McArdle, Executive Director,
Joshua's Place Healing Center

"We all yearn to know what our true calling is. In this beautiful book, Diane shares the magic and mystery of her journey and her awakening as a healer. What could be more inspirational?"

—Nancy Reuben, M.D., physician, healer and author of
Self-Care & Self-Empowerment Through Energy Awareness CD Series

"After I finished reading, I lay down and closed my eyes. The angels came and you were there. I had a healing of a pain that had been bothering me for years." — Karen Flynn, administrator and clairvoyant

"An amazing spiritual journey. Diane has gone through the fire."

—Laurie Campbell, medium and costar of
Discovery Channel's "Sensing Murder"

"Whether you're interested in alternative medicine, energy healing or one woman's unique journey, *A Call to Heal* is a fascinating book. It will stick with you long after you read it."

—Michael Gerber, *London Times* bestselling author.

"The early part of Diane Goldner's spiritual journey in *A Call to Heal* is punctuated by doubt. As the subtle nature of her transformation from journalist to healer becomes evident, we are swept up in it along with a loving assurance that a shift 'into the light' is available to us as well; if we look inward for the path we will see it. That is the great power of this beautiful book."

—Karen Kelly, author of *The Secret of the Secret: Unlocking the Mysteries of the Runaway Bestseller*

A CALL TO HEAL

A CALL TO HEAL

DIANE GOLDNER

GOLDEN SPIRIT BOOKS, LLC
NEW YORK • LOS ANGELES

Golden Spirit Books, LLC
P.O. Box 581
Santa Monica, CA 90406

First Golden Spirit Books edition 2013

For information about special bulk purchases, contact
Golden Spirit Books at 310-264-1924
or GoldenSpiritBooks@gmail.com.

Cover and book design by Randall Leers
Cover Photograph by Gia Canali

Library of Congress Control Number: 2013939704
ISBN # 978-1-940044-00-2

Salutations to
the Enlightened Teacher,
who by the power of
Self-knowledge, burns up
all the karmas acquired
through countless lifetimes.

———

THE SKANDA PURANA

Preface

ANY PEOPLE WHO have a healing ask: *How do you do this?* This book is an attempt to answer the question of how healing works. I also hope that the experiences I share will inspire you on your unique path.

I never intended to become a healer. I was a journalist, and a rather ambitious one, with no thought for higher realms. My unraveling began quite unexpectedly, when an article I wrote for *The New York Times* led to an initiation by an Indian master into the ultimate spiritual mysteries. After that awakening, a fire swept through my life, burning everything in its path. My life, as I knew it, fell apart. And I awoke to the inner light and its power to heal.

Along the way, I gave up my career, my status and many friends; in short, a way of life and my very identity. A healer's training is at least as rigorous as an elite athlete's, but it was my soul rather than my body that had to be developed. As my life dissolved, I was sure I would never be able to put it back together. Once I connected to the light, however, everything was so much better. I could not go back to the way things were. Nor would I want to. I only wish I could have discovered this domain earlier. So if this book opens a door for you, all the better.

Energy healing works with what we think of as spiritual energy. I also think it will be the basis of future medicine, after scientists learn more about this energy. But we don't have to wait. The light is available right now. It has been used for healing in cultures around the world for thousands of years.

Many people offered me healing light during my transformation. Now I am grateful to be able to hold light for others. With the power of subtle energy, I've seen miracles on an ongoing basis, things like arrhythmia, blood clots, pain and many other problems resolve. I've helped women who had been infertile get pregnant. I have witnessed dramatic recoveries from major surgery. I've supported cancer patients through physical, emotional and spiritual challenges. I've even watched as business deals were transformed by healing energy.

Ultimately healing energy is a balm for the soul. Because the soul and the body are intimately connected, the subtle energy helps people on all levels. We aren't merely physical beings. Consider these experiences:

"When you did the last healing, I could feel my heart open," wrote Kim in a note after her third long-distance session. "The only way I can describe it is like when the Grinch has that little heart and then it grows and grows all of a sudden . . . I have been aware in the past that I was closed off, but I didn't realize it could ever change."

———

When Delilah, a married woman with a young child, came to me for a few sessions, she didn't expect miracles. She just wanted to stay healthy. Her treatments for breast cancer had put her into premature menopause; a side effect that is typically permanent. But after three or four sessions in which I restored vitality and inner peace, her menstrual cycle returned, along with her fertility. "I don't know what you do," she said, "But it works."

———

Neil, an 8-year-old boy, lay in a coma in a hospital when his neighbors called to ask for help. Playing hide and seek on the roof of his apartment building, he had fallen three stories to the pavement below.

When I connected with Neil soul to soul, I saw that his energy field was shattered and frozen in fear. Working long distance, I transmitted the highest, most soothing light. I had to be ever so gentle and patient. After more than an hour his heart relaxed and came to rest in my heart. Finally I turned to his brain, gently adding healing light and restructuring the energy grid on which his brain cells grew. Very slowly the enormous pressure and pain in his head began to subside.

For the next week, Neil was agitated as the panic I cleared left his physical system. His doctors kept him in an induced coma, and after two weeks, allowed him to wake up. Soon, Neil was talking, laughing and smiling. Within weeks, although still fragile, his doctors declared him whole and sent him home.

———

Henrietta was facing extensive abdominal surgery known as a whipple. We did five sessions leading up to her surgery. At first the energy was grey and stagnant. I wasn't sure how well the surgery would go. After the first two sessions, the energy began to move. Finally during the last healing, it became ecstatic and extraordinarily dynamic. I knew then that the surgery would go very well.

During the operation there was almost no bleeding, and the surgeon found he had to do less cutting than normal. When the pathology report came back, it turned out Henrietta had a less aggressive cancer than expected, and a better life prognosis.

After surgery I continued to do healings for Henrietta. She was off pain killers in no time. Within ten days, her surgeons declared that her recovery was weeks ahead of schedule. Although part of her stomach had been removed, she was eating normally within a month.

———

Clive, who had metastasic cancer, said to me during one of our sessions, "I understand now that I have a soul." When he passed, he was completely at peace. His wife told me his passing was as mystical an experience as when she gave birth to their child.

———

Sam, a four-month-old baby, had been colicky since birth and allergic to his mother's milk. Nothing could soothe him, and eating always upset his intestines. I asked his mother if anything unusual had happened during her pregnancy. It turned out that shortly before giving birth, she had been in a car accident. Neither mother nor son had been injured and doctors had given them a clean bill of health. Yet in a healing session I saw that Sam was still in a state of shock. I cleared the fear from him and reconnected him to his mom. "He's not perfect. But it's like night and day," his grateful mother told me just a week later.

———

The vitreous fluid in Jason's eye had liquified, causing his retina to detach. "At that point," Jason recalls, "I had no idea if I would see again. I was literally in the dark." Doctors performed emergency surgery but they couldn't guarantee the result.

As I transmitted healing light from a distance, I saw that he was in a dark place emotionally and spiritually. I ran very high frequencies for healing into his eye and showed his soul how beautiful life could be.

"Fifteen or twenty minutes into the healing, I suddenly felt flooded by calm and well-being. It was absolutely tremendous," Jason recalled later. "I had been in a very bleak place before that. Suddenly I had the sense that everything was going to be all right. It was very tangible. And since then everything has worked out very well."

His eye healed and so did his life. "I didn't expect life to get so much better, but it has. Work has come back. And I'm back to being an optimistic person."

———

Gladys, a divorced woman in her 60s, had surgery to put a pin in her cancer-ridden thighbone. I met her in the recovery room where she was moaning softly from the pain. Gently placing my hand on her thigh, I added white light to help her cells rejuvenate. Sensing a deep loneliness, I also let her know through the energy that she was loved. A few days later, Gladys told me she had slept peacefully all night. She never needed a morphine drip. "I don't know what you did," she said. "But it helped. Thank you."

THESE ARE SOME of the many things that happen through the power of the healing light.

Author's Note

ALL OF THE events in this book happened as reported. To protect and honor people's privacy, I have changed names, along with other identifying information, in the healings and many of the experiences I describe.

I have also respected the wish of my Teacher, who prefers to remain anonymous. If this book kindles the desire in your heart for initiation, you will find your own true Teacher. Each of us has an enlightened Teacher in our very own innermost heart. The true purpose of a Teacher is simply to bring us home to the light and the bliss in our own heart.

Contents

Initiation

My World Falls Apart

Seeing Into The Spirit Realms

Gifts Of The Spirit

A Call to Heal

INITIATION

Prelude

I STILL REMEMBER the question Warren Beatty, the Academy Award winning actor and director, asked me one evening when we were on the phone, before he agreed to an interview for *USA Weekend*. His question summed up so much that I couldn't articulate for myself at that time.

"What are you going to do after you interview me?" Beatty asked, as we chatted on the phone.

By then I had zigzagged from investigative journalism and business exposés to feature writing. I had analyzed merger & acquisition strategies for an exclusive newsletter targeted to investment bankers, and written about some of the top lawyers in the country. Whatever I did, I did well. Yet I had changed my focus from features to business to investigative reporting, and back again, always sure the grass was greener somewhere else, and I would be happier and more successful.

Many of the journalists I had grown up with were now busy scribbling away at *The Wall Street Journal* and a few were even at *The New Yorker*. And here I was about to write my first celebrity cover story. I was excited about this new turn of events in my career, but at the same time, deep down feeling more than a little lost.

So when Beatty asked me that question, I answered honestly. "I don't know," I said. "Are you offering career advice?"

Beatty laughed. Then, almost before I knew it, I was driving into one of the most dramatic sunsets I had ever seen, as I took a series of hairpin turns up into the Hollywood Hills. When I had climbed as high as you could go, I turned into Beatty's driveway. We chatted for several hours that evening, and then we talked more over the next few weeks, and so began yet another chapter in my journalism career.

After writing about Beatty, I met with many other folks who were household names. I had the honor of meeting with talk show hosts Regis Philbin and Kathie Lee Gifford not once, but twice. I flew to Maine to interview novelist Stephen King and to Texas for a weekend with *Bridges of Madison County* author Robert James Waller. I even launched and edited a summer fiction series for *USA Weekend* showcasing short stories by bestselling authors. I became comfortable mixing and mingling with the *glitterati* and reporting on that scene.

I flew back to Los Angeles numerous times to meet with other well-known actors and actresses. Jean Claude van Damme, the action star, took off his shirt for me as he strutted by his pool, the better to show off his rippling muscles. Author Michael Crichton (of *Jurassic Park* fame) and I had a profound conversation about things both practical and metaphysical as we sat by a hotel pool in Santa Monica on a patio facing the ocean.

Some of these interviews and connections opened up new insights. Others reminded me that, like it or not, as a celebrity interviewer, I was basically a pawn in the publicity machine.

Still, I loved what I did. I couldn't dream of doing anything I would like more than journalism. People, and their unique and amazing lives, fascinated me. I also loved the written word and the magic it could make. Yet Beatty had voiced a question that lived within me somewhere deep inside.

Somehow, without knowing it, in all the corners of journalism I had explored, I was searching, unsuccessfully, for myself. By its very nature, it was a search that was doomed to failure. Perhaps I had an inkling that what I was seeking was outside of my grasp. Once, when I was working in a dream job as a senior editor overseeing business and investigative stories at a glossy late '80s magazine I thought, "*Could I really do this for the next 35 years? Is that really all there is to life?*"

It turned out that I would get quite an answer to these questions, an answer that I could never have imagined in a million years, an answer that nearly scared me to death—before saving my life.

CHAPTER I

Initiation

"**W**HY DON'T YOU come meet my Teacher?" Ingrid suggested over the phone. "It will change your life."

It was late 1993 and I had just profiled Ingrid, the founder of a charity focused on people with HIV and AIDS, for *The New York Times*. The story, one of the first I had written for the paper, ran on the front page of the Living Section. "You're such a good writer," my editor at *The Times* whispered breathlessly into the phone. My heart leaped. I was sure this meant good things for my career.

One good story often leads to another, I told myself as I contemplated Ingrid's invitation. It was obvious that Ingrid had been transformed by *something*, but I didn't see how it had anything to do with me. Still, she was inviting me to meet her Teacher, a meditation master from India. In Ingrid's view, the Teacher was illuminated and had the power to awaken the spiritual light in others. *A female meditation master? In the countryside outside New York City?* All I could think was: *What a great story!*

On New Year's Day 1994, I rode in Ingrid's van with Ingrid and her young daughter into the country. It was a cold, rainy, bleak day. I had been out the night before to ring in the New Year. I woke exhausted and dispirited. Each successive party had been more depressing than the previous one. It didn't matter that I had rubbed elbows with people who made the papers as "bold-faced" names. I hadn't had much fun. More troubling, I hadn't met anyone that I would want to date. I was now in my thirties and I was determined to find my perfect husband. Soon. I fully intended to have two children, like my parents before me.

At three a.m., bored and discouraged, I had gone home to my solitary apartment, a junior one-bedroom in Manhattan with a view of the Twin Towers, and put myself to bed. Now, in the car driving along the old-fashioned, tree-lined Palisades Parkway, I felt hung over even though I hadn't had a thing to drink. I had a queasy feeling, too, as I remembered the host of the first party. He was a well-known writer, the son of an industrialist and the very embodiment of Euro-trash style. I had been his editor at a previous magazine job.

I had never seen anyone quite so drunk. I knew that drinking was one of his main sources of amusement, second only to bedding down young women. He had tried to romance me, even though I wasn't quite his type. I had not been tempted in the least. *Could this really be the pinnacle of success?* I wondered, as I watched him, totally wasted. His behavior seemed utterly unappealing, and empty. I wondered how happy he could really be.

Lying in bed that morning, snuggled under my down quilt, surrounded by the flowering vines of the Laura Ashley wallpaper on my bedroom walls, I had considered ringing Ingrid to cancel. But I didn't like the idea of being alone; it was New Year's Day. It was too late to call a friend for brunch; besides the wait to get into a restaurant would be endless.

As Ingrid drove her minivan along the highway, I watched as we passed hill after hill of barren trees, naked in the dim winter light. There was something comforting about the stark grayness of the light; the landscape matched my mood.

Ingrid chatted merrily away, oblivious, it seemed, to my lethargic state. We stopped for gas. She bought donuts and coffee and offered me some of each, but I declined. *So that's what spiritual people eat?* I thought to myself. *Even I didn't eat donuts. Too fattening.* Being a New York editrix I always watched my waistline. I rarely wore skirts that came more than half way down my thigh. That day, however, I was wearing a green velvet dress that came to my knees and leggings; Ingrid had told me to dress modestly.

Finally we arrived at the ashram. We left the car in the muddy parking lot and marched along the walkway up to the entrance. It was even colder and damper up in the country. The sky seemed like it wanted to cry, but couldn't.

Once inside, we walked through the lobby and along the halls, all eerily empty. Ingrid led me to the main hall. When she opened the door I stepped into a riot of color and an electric excitement. Hundreds, if not thousands, of people sat packed together on the expansive floor, with women dressed in saris and shawls and velvets and the men also wrapped in shawls of every color.

Acres away, at the front of the room, on a wide chair, sat the Teacher. She wore the orange robes of a monk. Yet she looked like a queen. I felt as if I had stepped out of reality and onto a movie set. She was breathtakingly beautiful. But perhaps it wasn't so much her physical features. When I tried to think of an actress who could play the Teacher, I couldn't think of anyone who could match her radiance.

Ingrid found me a seat on the floor and went off to sit further back. The Teacher was giving a talk. Although I found it interesting, I listened through a deepening fog. My state got dreamier and dreamier. Finally I nodded off into a black-velvet sleep while sitting cross-legged, without even a backrest. I dropped all the way into the soft comforting folds of that void.

I woke as the Teacher started to lead the group into meditation. The lights dimmed. Gratefully, I drifted back to sleep again. I was so very tired. The next thing I knew, a gong sounded. The lights came back up.

Soon a long line of people formed in front of the Teacher. I watched as, one by one, people kneeled and bowed down to her. They acted as if she had something magical and precious that she could bestow on them, if only they could win her favor. I felt sad for them.

The Teacher sat serenely on her chair, unaffected by the frenzy of excitement and longing around her. She gently waved her hand over each person's head. She swept from right to left, tapping each person as she went. Then she swept back the other way. A beautiful, haunting song played in the background. Everyone moved as if in a dream.

"Come," Ingrid said, gently taking my arm. "I'll introduce you to the Teacher."

I shook my head. "I can't," I told her. "I would never bow down to anyone." *This is how it must have been around Jesus*, I thought to myself as I watched. *I would have walked away from the frenzied crowds, not believing. How did I get myself into this?*

"Why don't you think of it as bowing to your own higher Self?" Ingrid suggested.

Nice try, I thought to myself as I watched the tableau before me, riveted by the unabashed devotion and faith. *Were they all deluded? How could such a thing happen?*

Then the voice in my head began chiding: *Some reporters go to war. All you have to do is kneel down. How hard can that be? Where is your courage? Your spirit of investigation?*

"Okay, I'll go," I told Ingrid.

She escorted me to the front of the line. She stopped to speak to a perfectly groomed American girl who was wearing a very fine silk sari. Before I knew it, a space opened up for us in front of the Teacher. Ingrid and I knelt and bowed down directly in front of her.

Ingrid introduced me and told the Teacher about the article I had written. The Teacher nodded faintly at me. I nodded back. I felt like a deer trapped in the headlights of an oncoming car, completely frozen. It was as if my brain had stopped working. *Why was I so flushed with heat? Did I have a fever? Why couldn't I think? Or speak?*

Next to me, Ingrid chatted merrily. "Mmm," the Teacher murmured to Ingrid as she swept her hand over the tops of the people kneeling in a cluster before her. Her hand brushed my head a few times. She seemed utterly disengaged. Why did Ingrid continue? Didn't she see that the Teacher didn't care?

All of a sudden, our audience was over. No one said anything. Nevertheless, Ingrid and I got up at the same time.

As we walked away, someone tapped me on the shoulder. Ingrid, ahead of me, continued on as I turned around. Before me stood another beautiful young girl dressed in a luxurious silk sari. She held out a small box in her hands.

"This is a gift from the Teacher," the girl said. "She wants you to have this."

I hesitated. *A gift? For me? There were so many people. Why would the Teacher be giving a gift to me?*

The girl stood patiently, waiting for me to take it. Finally, I thanked her and took the gift.

It was a small woven box beautifully tied with a red ribbon and, in the spirit of the season, decorated with a sprig of plastic holly berries. *What kind of gift would the Teacher give me?*

I loosened the ribbon and pulled off the lid to find an assortment of fine chocolates. They looked absolutely delicious, but my heart sank; I worried they would make me fat. I rejoined Ingrid and started giving chocolates to Ingrid's daughter and her friends, feeling lighter with each one I handed out. Ingrid grew increasingly upset.

"Put those away," she finally ordered. "That's a gift from the Teacher. It has her energy, her *shakti*, her power. It's for you. Don't give any more away. When you get home, you must put them in your freezer. When you need help, take a little bite of the chocolate."

I had never heard anything so crazy. I thought Ingrid was joking, but she wasn't. Still, she was so insistent, I put them away.

WE SPENT THE rest of the day walking between one building and the next, taking our shoes off and putting them back on. I saw more mud than I had seen in a long time. We had lunch. We had tea. Ingrid asked me to wash a few dishes in the dish room to contribute something, and so I did.

We stopped to talk to people that Ingrid knew. I always stood back, politely waiting. They were all so excited to see Ingrid, to hear her news, to compliment her on *The New York Times* story. Even though I had written the article, I stood in the background, essentially invisible.

We had dinner with some of Ingrid's friends, and one of the men gave me a beautiful red rose, without seeming to want anything in return. Everyone was so nice. These friends of Ingrid's definitely weren't New Yorkers, at least, not the type that I knew. I couldn't put my finger on exactly what was different. But I did feel very welcomed.

After an exhausting day that seemed to last three weeks, we walked back to the parking lot. Night had fallen and it was so dark we could hardly see. We got into Ingrid's van to return to Manhattan. I shivered in the cold, wrapping my black wool coat more tightly around me.

As Ingrid started the engine, I turned to her and blurted out accusingly,

"I'm no different than I used to be."

My bitterness surprised me. I had had no illusions when I had agreed to come. *Why was I so upset now?*

"Why don't you wait and see?" Ingrid suggested brightly. "You know you fell asleep. I saw you nodding out. That's a sign that the *shakti,* the energy, is working."

Ingrid's enthusiasm grated on me now.

"I was just tired," I said.

I closed my eyes to nap. But suddenly I was wide-awake. So I pretended to sleep. I knew one thing: I wouldn't be pitching this story to anyone. I didn't have the heart to write about people who were so deluded.

When I got home, I put the chocolates in the freezer. I told myself I would save them for special treats. I nibbled on those chocolates for a long time.

CHAPTER 2

A Flame in My Heart

I WAS STILL FEELING bitter about New Year's Day when, a few days later, Ingrid called. She skipped right over my resentment and started schooling me in meditation. She introduced me to a mantra, a short string of Sanskrit words. "Just repeat the mantra as you breathe in, and again, as you breathe out," she instructed, explaining that the words would bring me inward. She told me to sit with my eyes closed and spine straight, either cross-legged on the floor or in a chair with my feet on the floor.

I had learned to meditate as a college freshman, on a visit to a friend who had dropped out of school and moved to a Zen Center. She had been rather unattractive, but after months at the Zen center she looked much prettier. That made me curious about meditation.

I can still remember the perfect order of everything at the Zendo. I was especially struck by how we had to clean our dinner bowls with warm tea after we ate, drinking the hot liquid along with any food we had left over. No soap and water needed, and no waste. Everything you put on your plate, you consumed. I also remember how I could barely walk after doing 108 prostrations to the Buddha each morning. Yet, as much as I liked the teachings and the simplicity, I found meditation unbelievably boring. I quit the practice after a few weeks. I never thought I would try it again.

It was different this time around. I couldn't say why. I found myself meditating every day. It was a compulsion. I simply had to meditate. I would feel restless and unresolved until I meditated. Then I would feel much better. I was going through a very stressful time and feeling quite anxious. Yet when I took the time to go inward, I often experienced a quiet bliss at the center of my being. Afterwards that sense of peace from the meditation would be there deep inside, like a flame in my heart. I had never experienced anything like it in my life.

At the time I thought my anxiety was largely the result of my work circumstances. I'd been freelancing for several years. When I made the decision to freelance, it seemed like the right thing. I thought it would help me discover what I really wanted to write about.

Since I was a young child I had always wanted to be a writer. From the moment I had learned to read, books had given me so much pleasure. They intimately connected me to other people, other worlds. Writing also seemed like the gateway to adventure, and a way to touch the human condition. Perhaps I hungered to write because I hungered to live and to connect deeply to others. For me it was also a way to go inward and find out what I truly felt and thought.

I especially loved fiction, followed by the biographies and autobiographies of people who had led interesting or unusual lives. Although I had written my share of short stories, I chose journalism as my career. I thought it would give me the best training as a writer. I found that I enjoyed interviewing and reporting as much as I liked to write. Yet somehow, as much as I developed my craft, I hadn't found what it was that I truly wanted to write about.

I had been promoted rather quickly up the masthead of several magazines, and wrote less and less as I became more senior. In this new freelancing phase, my writing flourished. It's when I began writing cover stories for *USA Weekend*, the Living and TV sections of *The New York Times,* and other publications. Nevertheless, there was always uncertainty about what assignment was coming next, and anxiety about money. Plus freelancing only exacerbated the feeling that I still hadn't found the right place for me. My ambition had no clear direction, yet could never be sated. I often asked myself: *What had I been thinking?*

As for the rest of my life, the things I had assumed would just naturally happen, like marriage and children, hadn't. I attracted my share of suitors. I just somehow never felt as if I had found the right fit with anyone. No one had told me that life didn't come with a guarantee. But I was finding that out.

Soon after graduating college, I had come close to marrying an ambitious young media executive who had success stamped all over him. He was a very smart, devoted and kind boyfriend, who also enjoyed managing and guiding my budding career. Everyone in my family had been waiting for us to announce our engagement and set a date for our wedding. But as much as I respected him and longed for the security of marriage, I didn't think we were happy enough together and I was sure we would end up divorcing. Now I wondered if I had made a mistake, searching for something that didn't exist. *Why couldn't I just get along, like everyone else?*

Meditation comforted me even when nothing else seemed to help.

CHAPTER 3

Subtle Shifts

"THE TEACHER IS a wish-fulfilling tree," Ingrid told me each time she called to check on me, which she did every so often. She basically had only this one message: "The Teacher is great; she is going to make everything in your life so much better. "

To strengthen her case, Ingrid recommend various books, including *Autobiography of a Yogi*, written by Paramahansa Yogananda. I found it interesting to read about meditation and the inner light and the power of an enlightened teacher. I felt that the author's mystical experiences were real.

Still I remained confidant that the meeting with the Teacher was a bust. Enlightened teachers might exist in earlier times, in faraway places like India, but certainly not in the tri-state area in the late 20th century.

In truth, I still knew almost nothing about meditation masters or how they worked. I had no idea, for instance, that one of the Teacher's primary purposes is to awaken her students to their inner knowingness. Nor did I know what that meant, even as the results of this unfathomable grace began to slowly manifest itself in my life.

It is only looking back that I can see that something began to shift in my life, even before I met the Teacher, as if time isn't as linear as we think. It was as if certain things were being set up for a total sea change, because just before I met the Teacher, the metaphysical began to seep into my life in the most unexpected ways, like water leaking in through the cracks. It was almost as if I was being prepared.

For instance, around the same time I interviewed Ingrid, *USA Weekend* had flown me to Los Angeles to interview bestselling author Michael Crichton (of *Jurassic Park* fame). A Harvard-trained medical doctor, Crichton claimed he could see auras. If a doctor could see auras, I thought, maybe they are real. But Crichton couldn't tell me much about them, just that he could see a subtle light around people. Still, his experience piqued my interest.

There was something else about that interview that stood out. The magazine had tapped several writers, none of whom could take the assignment, before they called me. I had the weird feeling that the meeting had been reserved for me.

Even the interview with Ingrid had, in a sense, been set up several years earlier, when I profiled a high society matron. She volunteered on the board of the charity that Ingrid had founded. This woman was often photographed modeling her latest designer frocks. But over the phone Ingrid gave a different picture of the woman, saying something that reverberated for a long time. *"She gives her time,"* Ingrid had told me. *"Our time is the only thing we can never get more of."* I had never thought of time as the most precious thing we are given. It was a sobering thought that continued to echo in my psyche. Some three years later, I remembered that conversation and proposed the story on Ingrid.

Around the time I began the *Times* story on Ingrid, I also began to study chemistry and physics. I simply woke up one morning and decided, out of the blue, that I had to register for chemistry at Hunter College. I hightailed it up to Hunter just in time to enroll during late registration. I thought I might write about medicine or even go to medical school. I soon changed my mind about medical school, but these science courses would come in handy as I researched the science of subtle energy, what the Chinese call *chi*, or life force.

T HOSE MOMENTS OF synchronicity, of protection, of guidance, seemed to accelerate. All of a sudden, changes started to take place ever so naturally, organically. I attributed the changes to my own doing. Nevertheless, as these new influences seeped in, things that weren't serving me began dissolving.

The first thing that went was my reliance on therapy. It would have been hard not to try psychotherapy. In artsy New York it was a cultural thing— think Woody Allen. Growing up in eastern Queens, in a simple, one-story brick house, the drinking water was practically spiked with the theories of Freud. When I was still a young child my mother, a social worker, went back to school to become a Freudian psychoanalyst. An uncle was one of the top psychoanalysts in the country and editor of the leading psychoanalytic journal. My aunt was a psychologist. Two out of three of my cousins would become therapists as well.

Growing up in a secular Jewish family headed by my dad, an accountant, there was plenty of talk about the stock market, psychoanalysis, and literature. But God and metaphysical questions were not part of the discussion in my immediate family, or in the sprawling network of aunts, uncles, grandparents and cousins on my mother's side. We skied on winter weekends, and spent summer afternoons by the ocean. The only time I stepped foot into the synagogue was on the holiest days of the year. My father's family was more observant, but in a way that seemed stifling and rote to me.

Reading was emphasized, just not holy books or books with a metaphysical cast. Still, books opened all kinds of doors for me, giving me insight into people and the world, and bringing a deep sense of connection and companionship. I wrote my first short story when I was just eight. And I was a voracious reader, roaming across time and space through books.

Once, as a teenager, my mother found me reading the "Seth" books, written by the artist Jane Roberts, who claimed to channel a high being named Seth. I was mesmerized by the explanations of the esoteric nature of reality and the laws of karma and consciousness. "Why are you reading junk like that?" My mother chided. I promptly abandoned the books.

In line with family tradition, I had gone to therapy for years, beginning in college. I hoped to fix my anxiety and the feeling I had deep at my core that something wasn't right. At first, the process had been an anchor. But for the last several years it seemed that therapy only sapped my time and finances. Yet I couldn't end it. I didn't have the therapist's blessing. The sad truth was I didn't trust myself.

One day, a month or two after my meeting with the Teacher, and much to my own surprise, I was done. I went for one final session to let my therapist know that I wouldn't be seeing her again. She almost fell out of her chair when I announced my decision. "Don't you want to talk about it?" she asked.

"No. We've already discussed it. For several years," I pointed out. "I know that you think I'm not done. If you are right, I can always come back." I didn't know why this reasoning had never occurred to me before. It seemed so very obvious.

SOON THE CONCEPT of subtle energy knocked on my door rather directly when a girlfriend set me up with a psychiatrist. The setup didn't lead to a romance, but it wasn't long into the evening when my date pulled out a big book from his shoulder bag. "Here, take a look at this," he said with excitement. It was an odd book for a psychiatrist: *Hands of Light*. To my mind, it seemed more like something a shrink might use to commit someone.

To be polite, I took the book from him. Scanning the pages I saw pictures of people surrounded by energy fields, and of healers surrounded by spirit guides. Despite myself, I was riveted, like someone looking at photos of nudes who had never before seen a naked body.

The text gripped me, too. The author, Barbara Brennan, a former NASA scientist, asserted that illness began in an invisible energy field around and in the body, when energy became congested or leaked. Further, she claimed that many illnesses can be healed by changing the energy. It was all a matter of the healer holding a high vibration. The ill person would absorb the new energy state, just the way one crystal glass begins to resonate with another. Brennan wrote that healing in this manner was easier and more effective for many things.

Could this be true? I wondered. *If so, wouldn't I already know about it? Wouldn't it be common knowledge?* After all, I read as many as four newspapers a day and had gone to an Ivy League college. I had never heard even a whisper about energy healing. On the other hand, when presented as if it was an aspect of physics, it made sense. If it was real, the implications were enormous. Imagine if there was an easier, more direct way to heal. News of such a thing would surely be quite a scoop.

As I skimmed the book on healing, I recalled the meeting I had with the Teacher. I had been so sure that nothing had happened. Now, in the back of my mind, I wondered: *Could there have been some kind of shift through this resonance? Was that why I was having such great meditations?*

As I held the book in my hand, I made a mental note of the title and the author. I vowed to find a magazine to assign me a story on the subject. I would find out if healing energy was real or not.

I had no idea how naive and ignorant I was, which was probably a good thing.

CHAPTER 4

A Wish-Fulfilling Tree?

EIGHT MONTHS AFTER meeting the Teacher, I thought everything in my life was coming together. I had begun dating a new man; things had taken off rather quickly. My new beau and I seemed to have so much in common, especially as we were both writers and kindred spirits. I believed love conquered all.

My career also seemed to be coming up roses. I was laying the groundwork for an investigative story about healing for a body/mind magazine, *New Age Journal*. Plus, my editor at the *Times* referred me to a copyediting job at *The Wall Street Journal*, the same job she once had. It was a paper I had dreamed about writing for since I was a child, reading my father's copy at the kitchen table after school. I wasn't too keen on copyediting. But it was just part-time and it was a foot in the door. Besides, it would give me stability while I freelanced.

And to top it all, I got a plum assignment with the Sunday *Daily News*. They wanted me to write a weekly society column, attend black tie dinners, premieres, openings and celebrity birthday parties with New York's *glitterati*. I said yes without a backward glance. I couldn't believe my good fortune.

By day I was a scribe in the back offices of the *Journal*. By night, I rubbed elbows with NY's elite, nibbled on blini hors-d'oeuvres and gourmet dinners, and toted home little party-favor bags. My evenings were a whirlwind of opening-night galas, benefits and small private dinners with masters of the universe. It was my job to sit and chat with the famous, the infamous, the talented, and the super rich. Every night I talked with network executives, actors, directors and billionaire Wall Street tycoons. Afterwards, their glittering *bon mots* appeared in my column, along with their bold-faced names.

Publicists put me at A-list tables, where I sat next to people who were on television and in the movies, and then called the next morning to make sure I had had a good time. Suddenly everyone wanted to be my friend. It was a bit fluffy and unreal, with a few genuine moments mixed in to keep me sane. Still, it was a great front-row seat onto society.

My life wasn't perfect, but I had mysteriously manifested a version of everything I thought I wanted. *Was the Teacher a wish-fulfilling tree?* I concluded that it was just the normal turnings, nothing mystical at all. But life seemed to be filled with wonderful adventures.

CHAPTER 5

A Skeptic Investigates

"REACH OUT YOUR hands and extend your fingers to the ceiling," healer Barbara Brennan instructed at the introductory workshop in late August 1994.

I had begun the research for my magazine story on energy healing. At Barbara's request, I started by attending her course, held at a hotel on Long Island and over 100 people had signed up for it. All around me, people reached their hands toward the ceiling. I copied them, so that I wouldn't stand out. Of course, I didn't feel the ceiling with my fingertips from 20 feet away. Who in their right mind would?

Barbara had us do a few other elementary exercises. I wasn't any better at feeling "energy" in these exercises. As far as I could tell, this energy was turning out to be mighty imaginary. I felt relieved—it's nice to have one's worldview confirmed—but also a little disappointed.

Next, Barbara asked us to pick a partner and take turns doing hands-on healings for each other. She did a healing for all of us to see so we would know where we should put our hands.

I found myself teamed with a very nice young man. He told me that his father had died of a degenerative illness, but he had no physical complaints. Just my luck! I thought. I'm not going to get any "good" experience here. Still, I did the healing. The only thing I noticed was that he was wonderfully healthy. He was so robust! I wondered if he felt guilty for being so incredibly healthy when his father had degenerated before his eyes. I knew in my heart that this man's father would never have wanted his son to be sick.

"You're so healthy," I said, when I finished. "It's wonderful. And, you know, I hope you're not feeling guilty that you're healthy and your father was not, because you shouldn't. It's a wonderful gift. He would be very happy."

He thanked me for the healing. He said he did sometimes feel guilty for being so healthy, but he would let that guilt go now. It was only years later that I realized this young man did receive a healing—absolution from "the sin" of being healthy when his father was not.

Subtly, a door had opened, although I didn't quite realize it yet. My boyfriend fantasized that perhaps one day I would heal him of a chronic condition that he had. But at the same time, he seemed ever so slightly put off by the new drift of energy. Still I was back to writing exciting stories and I felt I had finally regained my balance. Things were happening again. While I began to feverishly read about healing energy, I enjoyed all the A-list parties, where I rubbed elbows with the New York's most powerful people.

Then, as quickly as everything had materialized, it all dissolved as if it had been nothing but a dream. *The Daily News* replaced me with a staff writer for budget reasons. Then I discovered I was pregnant. My boyfriend, who had loved going to all the parties with me, became cold and distant. He begged me to terminate the pregnancy that he had consciously initiated. Heart-broken, I did.

Some wish-fulfilling tree.

CHAPTER 6

Revelations

EALER BARBARA BRENNAN'S headquarters in those days was a house converted into an office in the town of East Hampton on Long Island. Light streamed through the big windows of her personal office, illuminating pictures of several modern-day saints from various traditions. The room boasted a big writing table and a cozy divan for meditation and contemplation. The shelves of books, which ran the entire length of the room underneath the windowsills, were most striking of all.

Barbara had quite a collection of books and scientific texts with a metaphysical orientation. I wanted to spend a few days among them, trying to learn everything I could. I was also eager to see if Barbara could be clairvoyant. The idea of such a gift transfixed me. It had always piqued my interest, ever since reading science fiction books as a child. I thought it would be wonderful to have such abilities, but never imagined that they could be real.

I found myself feeling a little nervous. *What if she was clairvoyant? What if she could somehow see my recent pregnancy and its abrupt end?*

Barbara gestured to a chair and I sat down. She broke the ice first. "So how did you decide to become a healer?" she asked, then caught herself. "I mean, a journalist."

"It's just a slip," I reassured myself, not daring to ask and find out

otherwise.

Barbara and I talked for several hours about healing and how she became a healer. "Are you going into Manhattan?" she asked when we concluded the interview.

"Yes," I said.

"Can I hitch a ride?"

"Of course," I said. As we headed west towards the city on the Long Island Expressway, the sun began to set. The sky turned a beautiful pink and orange. It was deep winter, when the world begins to darken in mid-afternoon, creating a more intimate atmosphere as we drove. I had asked Barbara many questions, always keeping my reporter's distance. Now I had a personal one that popped out of my mouth.

"When does the soul enter an unborn baby?" I asked. I was desperate for an answer to this one. I had just gone through one of the most devastating experiences, something I had sworn I would never let happen to me.

"Before conception," she said.

"Before conception? How can that be?"

She laughed gently. "It's an agreement between the mother, the father and the child," she explained. At the soul level, she added, time doesn't exist as it does for us in physical reality.

"I have a personal reason for asking." I didn't elaborate. It didn't matter. It was as if Brennan was inside my mind. I could almost feel her rummaging around for the relevant files.

"I know," she said. "I see your daughter. She is still very close to you. She's a lovely little girl. But you did the right thing. The father did not want the child, and you didn't need to bring rejection on you or the child."

I was stunned. During the few weeks that I had been pregnant I couldn't shake the feeling that I was carrying a girl. How could Brennan know? How could she guess that my boyfriend did not want the child?

Ending the pregnancy had been one of the hardest decisions I had ever made. Since then, I had been racked by grief, and by panic that, if there was a God, I might burn in hell forever.

"Now you have to ask yourself," Brennan continued, "why would you choose a man like that? " The question jolted me. I wanted to protest that I didn't know he was like *that*.

Barbara began speaking in a stilted, slower cadence. She said she was channeling Heyoan, her spiritual guide. "The child is fine," she said in her strange lilt. "She may even incarnate as your child again, with a different father. It will be the same soul, with different genetic ties."

I wanted this to be true more than anything. At the same time, I didn't know how to trust the prophecy. "This sounds like hokum to me, " I said.

"That's just one probable reality," Brennan said, still speaking in the odd cadence.

Strangely, whether Brennan's vision was accurate or not, my anguish lifted for the first time, and it never came back. Brennan did not lay hands on me. But it felt as if she had *seen* into my soul. And she had helped me see myself, and my situation in a new light.

Brennan shared other things that I wanted to know about, including some of her experiences with saints and spiritual masters. All in all, the few hours I spent with Barbara Brennan opened new doors. She had even gone to see the same Teacher that I had met. I knew because I had seen her picture in Brennan's office. "What is her aura like?" I asked, ever the reporter.

"You know what white light is?" she said. "Well, this is beyond even that." She went on to tell me how she had also visited the Temple at the retreat center. "I saw the most extraordinary blue light coming from the statue," she told me. "If you saw that light, you would bow down, too."

When I got home to my apartment, I marveled at how much lighter I felt. *How had all that pain dissolved?*

CHAPTER 7

Trouble in My Throat

REPORTERS OBSERVE. THEY note. Then, they move on. You peek through the window, yet you're always detached. It was a role I rather liked. I didn't realize how much I used it to protect myself.

There I was at the Barbara Brennan School of Healing, sitting in on a sophomore lecture. "First Chakra," Barbara called out from the stage to the 150 sophomores in her four-year school.

Chakras are described in Hindu, Tibetan and North American spiritual teachings as vortexes of energy located along the spine. They mediate the connection between the physical, emotional, mental and spiritual realms.

Brennan's students appeared to take her command seriously. But I couldn't see or feel a chakra if my life depended on it. "Second chakra," Barbara ordered a minute later. And so it went. *How could I assess this?* I wondered. It seemed so imaginary. Not much time elapsed before Barbara called out, "Fifth Chakra."

All of a sudden, my throat began to burn. Tears welled up in my eyes from the pain. I wanted to flee before I choked to death. Frantically, I looked around for an escape. I saw the exit sign, but it was so far away I would never make it. *What was going on?* Suddenly, a thought flashed. *Fifth chakra. Wasn't that the throat?* At that, my throat opened up. I could breathe.

When the class ended, the teacher chaperoning me explained that I had an energy block in my throat and it reacted to all the fifth chakra energy. I vaguely remembered the fifth chakra had to do with issues of speaking and creativity and manifesting. How could I, a writer, have issues there? "That's ridiculous," I told the healing teacher, more than a little angry.

The message was repeated when I had dinner with Gerda Swearengen. A German woman who had married a career American Army officer, Gerda had a no-nonsense, efficient and direct style. After she asked a question during the class I had attended, I knew I had to talk to her. Her words in class *lit up*.

At dinner, I showered her with questions about healing. Gerda was very forthright, generous with her knowledge, and patient with my inquisition. Finally, she turned to me. "The energy in your throat is so constricted it almost looks as if you have a noose around your neck," she observed.

My throat, again. "That's impossible." I said, trying to hide how upset I felt.

"I'll release the energy for you," she offered. After a moment's hesitation I agreed to let her give it a try. I told myself she had to be making it up. I wanted to see how she would spin it.

After dinner, we found a secluded corner of the hotel lobby. As I stood in front of her, Gerda waved her hands here and there about my neck. I was about to gleefully exclaim, "See!" at the futility of her efforts. Just then a little whoosh of air released from somewhere deep in my chest and throat, and out through my mouth. It happened so fast it took me by surprise. Gerda looked very pleased with herself.

I didn't know what to think.

B Y THE TIME I finished the magazine article, I knew there was something to healing energy. In the course of my reporting, I interviewed people who had made dramatic recoveries. One woman had macular degeneration, a condition where the macular part of the retina develops a hole, which generally gets bigger over time. There is no known medical cause, and it is considered irreversible.

In this case, the woman told me that after a series of healings, the subtle channels feeding energy to her eyes had been cleared of blockages. All I knew for sure was that the hole in one of her retinas *disappeared* and the hole in the other eye had gotten smaller. I never would have believed it, except that her doctors had medical records and images to prove it.

In another case, which Gerda handled, a woman had broken her pelvis. Nine months later, it hadn't healed and she was confined to a wheelchair. After a few healings, memories of having been sexually abused in her childhood surfaced; her bones began to knit together. Soon, she was walking. And Gerda was "just" a student.

Then the professor in the physics class I was taking at Hunter College, a retired Coast Guard captain, gave a lecture one day in which he discussed the power of energy frequencies. To illustrate, he showed a short film of a suspension bridge built in Tacoma, Washington, in 1940. All the steel parts resonated at the same frequency—an engineering error. One day the wind just happened to hit that frequency. The bridge fell apart in one long wave as if it was made of matchsticks. (You can watch this mesmerizing footage on YouTube.)

"Everything has a frequency. Even you," the professor concluded, turning the projector off.

"What did you mean?" I asked when I went to see him in his office. I confessed that I was trying to make sense of some books about chakras and healing energy.

"It's all real," he said, much to my surprise, adding, to my further astonishment, that he had been studying the chakras for years. He told me that the way to understand the subtle realm was through quantum physics. He urged me to read *The Dancing Wu Li Masters*. The book showed how things are connected beyond time and space in the quantum domain which, he asserted, was also the way things work on the spiritual planes.

I had so many questions. Why not get the answers by writing a book on energy healing? Non-fiction writers I admired had tackled subjects such as geological formation and the making of a skyscraper. Energy healing seemed a lot more interesting than those subjects. The first step would be to pull together enough material for a book proposal so I could get a publishing contract.

As part of my investigation, I would want to see what energy healing felt like from the inside. *Why not use myself as a guinea pig?*

CHAPTER 8

Visit to a Healer

DIANNE ARNOLD, a former general partner in a stock
brokerage firm, was a newly minted graduate of the Barbara
Brennan School of Healing. She had a sense of humor, a New
York accent, and a warm, comforting, down-to-earth style.
Her Brooklyn townhouse had lovely hardwood floors, big
windows and a comfy, somewhat worn couch. She even had a sweet white
poodle named Angel who barked just like a normal dog. Everything seemed
safe and ordinary.

Dianne sat me on the couch and asked me to tell her what I wanted to
focus on in the healing. I told her I wanted more clarity about my career.
I had been successful, but didn't know what my next step should be. Even
more than that, I admitted that I wanted to create a happy and fulfilling
relationship, leading to marriage.

I doubted there was much she could do. I had been through years of
psychoanalysis yet still had all the same issues. If anything, my confusion
seemed to get worse with each passing year.

In the first session Dianne said she would strengthen and straighten
my "hara" line, the aspect of our subtle anatomy that oversees intention
and purpose. I laid on her table and closed my eyes. Soon I noticed the
strangest sensation: something spinning inside of me, yet not in my body,
as if there was a vortex of energy that funneled out from my core. I opened

my eyes to see Dianne holding a pendulum over my abdomen, the location of the third chakra. I had read that chakras were vortexes of energy. But now I had experienced it. *Extraordinary!* It was my first tangible proof that chakras were real. The sensation of myself as a vortex of energy was rather pleasant. Still, by the end of the session, I wondered if I had made it up.

In the next session, Dianne described being guided to draw flowering vines on my "etheric" body. Whatever an "etheric" body was.

In the following session, Dianne told me she had worked with "snake" energy. When I got on the subway heading back to Manhattan, a girl darted in front of me and took the seat I had picked for myself. I took the one across from her. As she sat down, she crossed her legs, revealing a long tattoo of a snake. It started at her ankle, and twisted up her leg, with its head emerging at the underside of her knee. I was amazed. But it was the only effect I could track, so what good did that do?

In the fourth session, Dianne claimed four goddesses came and did the healing while she stood and "held the space." "Who were these Goddesses?" I asked suspiciously.

"Tara, the Buddhist goddess of healing," Dianne said. "Quan Yin, Mother Mary, and someone I've never heard of before." She cocked her ear, as if listening. "She says her name is Sweet Mother," Dianne reported.

I admired and even envied Dianne her poetic imagination. Still, where was the result in my life? Besides, why would a group of Goddesses come to visit *me*? I didn't believe Goddesses were real. And if they were, well, wouldn't they be busy doing something important? Why would they bother with me?

Finally, I came for what I assumed would be my fifth and last session. As we sat on the couch talking, Dianne looked at me intently. Then she got up and turned on a lamp near me, squinting, as if to see something better. She sat back down and continued to study me in a way that started to make me uncomfortable. A moment later, she told me that she wanted to work on my neck.

"You have quills in your neck," she explained. *My neck, again.*

"You're speaking metaphorically, aren't you?" I asked.

"No," she replied. "There really are quills. Someone's been throwing barbs at you when you try to speak your truth. The quills are on the right side," she continued. "That means they were thrown by men."

I could accept quills as a metaphor. But I had never seen feathers with sharp shafts in my neck. Diane had seemed so normal, but this was too bizarre for me. I got up to leave. At the last minute, however, I got on her healing table. I told myself that I wanted to see what would happen, how she could pull such a ridiculous claim off. But perhaps some deeper part of me was guiding my choice.

I soon fell into that state of pleasant, slightly drugged relaxation I had come to associate with receiving healing energy. Then Dianne reached my neck. She didn't touch me; yet I could feel her hands rustling near by. I experienced the most irritating stinging sensation, as if needles or stingers were being twisted and removed.

"Whatever you're doing, that hurts," I said. The sensation was so annoying that I wanted to grab her hands and make her stop. Even so, I felt sure it was due to the power of suggestion.

"I'm just removing the quills," she said. "It'll be over in a minute."

"Are the 'quills' going to come back?" I asked, sarcasm in my voice, when she finished.

"Not unless you let them," Dianne said quietly.

I left Dianne's house convinced that I would never return.

TEN DAYS LATER, never having given the quills another thought, I got into a heated argument with a male relative. I couldn't believe how he was trying to control me. Suddenly, I heard the nasty condescending tone in his voice. I got very quiet. "You can't speak to me that way," I said. He became more furious, but I felt complete.

The next day I remembered the "quills." My relative had thrown a barb at me, and for the very first time in my life, I had noticed it. And I didn't let it stick. In some inexplicable way, I knew without a doubt those quills had been real.

In removing the quills, it was as if Dianne had gone in and reset my programming. *Subtle energy is real,* I thought. *It has real effects.* There was just one problem: If the energy was real, then so was the blockage in my fifth chakra, the energy center that oversees creativity, speaking, and manifesting. The idea made me queasy. What did it say about me as a writer?

"You have a lot to clear there," Dianne said gently when I asked her what it all meant. "Maybe that's part of what you came in to do. Maybe that's why you chose to be a writer, to make sure you clear these blocks. Right now, you're like a one-legged runner."

Great, I thought. *Things are even worse than I thought.*

My World Falls Apart

CHAPTER 9

The Divine Mother

A S I RECOUNTED the odd experiences I was having in my healing sessions, Kim, an old college acquaintance, became increasingly intrigued. I had run into Kim at an art opening, after not seeing her for nearly a decade. Now we were having dinner at a trendy Thai restaurant in Soho that had a thatched-roof décor. The place seemed to cater to super-thin models and their dates, except for Kim and me.

Kim, it turned out, had gone to see several healers herself since I had last seen her. She explained that shortly after graduating, she suffered head injuries in a car accident. She had even gone to Medjugorje in Yugoslavia, where a group of children had had visions of the Virgin Mary.

"You mean, the healer identified Sweet Mother, without knowing anything about her?" asked Kim, obviously impressed.

"Yes," I said. "Who is Sweet Mother?" I had always assumed she was a figment of Dianne's imagination. Kim seemed to think she was real.

"Sweet Mother was the consort of Sri Aurobindo, a famous yogi," Kim replied. She explained that Sweet Mother had foretold the coming of a Divine Mother, a woman who had grown up in India and now lived outside of Frankfurt in Germany, using the name Mother Meera.

"You must read the book, *Hidden Journey*," Kim urged. "Then you'll understand."

I went and got the book. I found *Hidden Journey* fascinating. I even counted how many times the author, Andrew Harvey, had seen Mother Meera in person. But it didn't convince me of anything. What got my attention was that Sweet Mother had come to me in that healing. How could something like that happen? I knew it was a sign that I had better take my sessions with Dianne seriously.

CHAPTER 10

A Tidal Wave of Energy

INGRID RANG ME up a little more than a year after my visit to the Teacher. "There's going to be a special chant. You must go," she said, very excited and emphatic, as only Ingrid could be.

"I don't think so," I replied.

"You must go to this chant," Ingrid persisted. "It's very important."

It turned out that the special chant was scheduled for a day when I had to be at *The Journal*. I was grateful to have such an easy excuse for skipping a visit to the ashram. I had no desire to ever go back.

"You could ask for time off," Ingrid suggested.

"I'll lose my job," I said.

"This is more important than your job," Ingrid said.

"I don't think so," I replied, annoyed. It was the only thing I had left to hang on to, like a lone tree on a wind-swept plain.

We were still going back and forth when my boss buzzed me. "Can you come down to my office?" he asked.

I got off the phone and hurried into my boss's office. He was a very polished, handsome, intelligent man who was also kind and decent. He was one of the most powerful editors at the paper, and had carved out his own domain where he reigned as king.

He started with the good news. "You're a fine reporter and writer," he said. Then he continued with the not-so-good news. "But we both know that you aren't crazy about copy editing. Your six-month trial period is almost up. I'm going to have to let you go. But I would like you to continue to write for my sections. That's what you really want to be doing anyway."

Stunned, I left his office. Now, even this job was gone.

"How auspicious," Ingrid said when I called back with the news. "Don't worry. This really is better than that job."

I felt the presence of a *force*. It *knew* that I didn't want this job and that I had put it in the way of going to the ashram. I could still resist this *force*: *But at what cost?*

I had nothing else to do. I agreed to go to the chant.

AT THE LAST minute, Ingrid said she couldn't join me and sent me to the ashram alone by bus. As soon as I arrived I knew I had made a mistake. I didn't know a soul. And I didn't want to be there.

It was too late to go back to New York that night. With resignation, I went to the dining hall and took some soup and brown rice. The food, so thin and boring, made me feel more lonely and out-of-place. I didn't know that the food was designed to be especially light and bland because of the events to come. There wasn't much else to do after dinner, so reluctantly I went to the chant.

When I opened the door to the hall, the chant enveloped me with an intensity that felt physical. The haunting sound rose and fell like the waves of the ocean. It was the middle of the winter. All of the frenzied crowds were gone. There couldn't have been more than a hundred people in the hall. They sat solitary along the walls and the tiered steps in shawls that covered their heads and bodies like shrouds. A strange heat radiated through the room.

The Teacher sat at the front of the hall in her chair. Her eyes were half-closed, as if she was looking inward. Yet it was her voice that filled the room and buoyed everyone. The lights were dim, as if we were enveloped in a sacred twilight blue.

I had only experienced such stillness, such sacredness, once before, when I lived in Rome as a college student. At the urging of a stranger I passed on a street, I opened a door and found myself staring at The Holy Steps, said to be the very same stairs, imported from Jerusalem, that Jesus climbed on the last day of his life. The faith emanating from that space, where people climbed the hard stone steps one by one on their knees in ardent prayer, was so powerful I wanted to weep.

In the hall I quietly took a seat on the floor. For the next several hours I chanted the mantra I had been using to meditate. I didn't know that this was the sacred holiday of *Mahashivaratri*, considered the most auspicious night to chant the mantra. The grace from each repetition is said to be amplified a thousand times.

At times, I couldn't believe I was chanting. Then I would become completely immersed. Sometimes a wave of emotion ran through me and I would cry about the sorry state of my life. Then my tears would dry and I would be riding on the chant once again.

The Teacher left the hall soon after midnight. I left, too. When I woke in the morning it was still too early for breakfast, so I returned to the hall. The Teacher was already there.

The all-night chant came to an end. All of the people in the hall lined up to kneel before her. I debated as to whether I would join the line; I didn't really see the point.

When in Rome, do as the Romans do, the voice in my head suggested. So I got in the line. As I knelt before the Teacher, she swept by me once, then twice, then three times. *Nothing.* I wouldn't be coming back again.

I got up to go. Yet something compelled me to turn around and face the Teacher. It was as if some force possessed me. I would never have done it myself.

"Thank you for everything," I said. The words popped out of my mouth quite unexpectedly, as if someone was speaking through me. *Why was I saying this?* I wondered. *Was I referring to my wonderful meditations?* I didn't think she had anything to do with that. *The jobs I had lost? The creep I had dated? The unexpected pregnancy? What exactly could I be thanking her for?* Why were these words coming out of my mouth when I didn't agree with them?

The Teacher's eyes pierced me. With great deliberation, she lifted her hand. "Oh, you are the writer," she declared as if she had been expecting me, could see every aspect of me. Her tone penetrated me to the bone.

Suddenly we were the only two people in the universe. She slowly brought her hand down towards the crown of my head. She never reached my actual head. But a wave of energy went through me with the force of a tsunami.

The wave reverberated through parts of me I had never felt. I suddenly understood I was far vaster than my physical body and extended much higher than my head. There was also nothing solid about me. The room faded. My world ended. Eternity enveloped me.

Then it was over. Once again, I had a physical body. I looked around. I saw the Teacher. She wouldn't catch my eye or acknowledge me. It was as if I didn't exist, as if that moment—the most extraordinary, inexplicable moment—hadn't happened. She just went on nodding and murmuring to those kneeling before her. I felt feverish and confused.

Had anyone seen what had happened? Had I just imagined the whole thing? No one seemed to notice anything.

Eventually I called Ingrid from a pay phone. Scrunched into the phone booth, I described what had happened.

"You've got it. You've got it," she said excitedly.

"Got what?" I said, still feeling shaken and damp with fever.

"*Shaktipat*," she replied. "Divine initiation. The awakening of the spiritual energy. The descent of Grace."

"Oh," I said. It still didn't make any sense.

It wouldn't make any sense for a very long time. But after that, just as Ingrid had predicted, my life did change. I didn't notice it at first. When you turn a large boat, it takes awhile to see that it is going in a new direction.

CHAPTER 11

The Recapitulation

"I WANT MY scarf back," I told Dianne.

After the experience with the "quill" healing, I had come back for some more sessions. If I was going to be writing a book, I needed to know how this energy worked from the inside. In truth, I hoped Dianne could help me sort a few things out. I didn't know exactly what they were, but I knew something wasn't working right in my life.

I had spent the last half-hour crying to her about the boyfriend who had gotten me pregnant. It had seemed, at least to me, that we were a perfect fit. But a few weeks before we broke up, he had traded scarves with me. I realized afterwards that this wasn't an accident. He had a raincoat from one girl. He had a pair of pajamas that had belonged to another girl's father. He had a hat from a third girl. I didn't want him having any souvenir from me. It gave me the creeps.

Almost any woman would have said, "good riddance to bad rubbish." Sadly, not me. I longed for everything to be all right. Dianne would talk some sense into me and I would leave her house feeling grateful that I was free of him. Then the longing to see him would start all over again.

I thought Dianne would tell me I should forget about my silly scarf. But she didn't. "You're right," she said. "You don't want him to have anything that belongs to you. It will keep you linked."

She looked at me keenly and fell silent, seeming to contemplate something. "I am going to teach you something that will help you get clear," she announced after a long moment, sitting up straighter on her couch, the one covered in a Chinese silk pattern. Her tone and her focus had suddenly become quite serious. Her dog, Angel, poked her nose in my tea. For once, Dianne didn't even notice Angel's bad table manners.

"This is strong medicine," Dianne continued. "You must treat it with great respect. Do you promise to do that?"

I sat up straighter, too. "Of course," I promised. I couldn't wait to receive the teaching.

"It's called the Recapitulation," Dianne explained. "I learned it from Taisha Abelar, one of the sorcerers connected to Carlos Castanada, the author who studied with Don Juan and wrote about his mystical teachings."

Wow, I thought to myself. *So Carlos Castanada was for real?* I had never read his books. I made a note to myself to start reading them, along with Taisha Abelar's book, *The Sorcerer's Crossing*.

"It's a shamanic technique," Dianne continued. As she explained, it basically involved turning my head from right to left as I breathed in, and then the other way as I breathed out. Then I was to do a "sweeping" pass, where I turned my head back and forth without any breath at all. Dianne told me that while I did this exercise, I was to recall one scene at a time from the relationship. When I breathed in, I'd be pulling all my energy and consciousness back to me from that scene. As I breathed out, I'd be returning this guy's energy to him. During the sweeping, I'd be erasing it all, wiping the slate clean.

"Start at the beginning of the relationship. Go through every single moment. It will take you some time," Dianne instructed.

"That's it?" I asked, incredulous.

"Yes," Dianne replied.

"You think a few simple breaths are going to break all the ties?"

"Why don't you just try it?" Dianne said gently but firmly. "Judge for yourself. See if it works."

A FEW DAYS LATER I went for a walk along the East River Park, a long skinny stretch nestled between the rush of the FDR Drive highway, and the grey, surging waters of the East River. It was not too far from my apartment and I often took long walks there, especially now that my *Journal* job had come to an end. It was a relief to leave my home office, where I always felt like I should be doing *something*. Several years earlier I used to jog that same path, doing four or five miles at a time. But now I liked the contemplative pace of walking.

After going about two miles along the water towards the Manhattan Bridge, I reached a grove of trees growing in a circle. I had walked past this group of trees hundreds of times without ever really seeing them. Now I noticed that they created a sacred, protective, almost magical space. This gave me the urge to sit down and try the Recapitulation. I zeroed in on one particular tree and sat down by it.

I took a meditative pose. As I called in the four directions and Grandmother Earth and Grandfather Sky, as Dianne had instructed, I felt silly. Yet I thought it best to follow her instructions precisely. She had told me it was very important to protect myself with the shamanic powers.

I began at the beginning of the relationship. As I breathed in the first scenes, I was stunned. This guy had been so difficult even on our first date. I had forgotten that I vowed not to see him again. He talked me into a second date. He pleaded and cajoled until I agreed to get together again. He even convinced me to come up to his neighborhood, breaking one of the rules I had for myself about first, second and third dates. I had completely forgotten these details, which now seemed so telling of what was to come.

I felt shaken when I got up from my session. I didn't like what I had seen. I had no backbone. I was too eager to please, too easily persuaded. Nevertheless, I didn't feel the exercise had accomplished all that much.

The next time I took a walk along the East River, I came upon the same grove of trees. Despite everything, I gave the recapitulation another try. As I sat there, breathing in and breathing out scenes from the relationship and sweeping those scenes clean, I noticed that something *was* happening: I was *seeing* myself.

What I saw shocked me. This guy may have treated me poorly, but he hadn't done so without my permission, implicit in the way I spoke and behaved. I had been blaming him. Yet I had been a willing participant. I had done so unconsciously, of course. I had been completely disconnected from the true, knowing aspect of myself. I had long taken pride in my level of self-awareness, so it was a sobering revelation.

I reported back to Dianne. She nodded approvingly. "That's good," she said. "You're doing great."

"Will this really free me?"

"You've *seen* yourself. You'll be more conscious." Dianne explained. She paused. "You know," she said. "You can do this recapitulation for your other relationships as well."

"What a great idea," I said. I was by now desperate to clear these patterns.

"There's just one thing you must promise me. Do not ever recapitulate your mother or your father. You will un-root yourself. If you do that, I will not work with you. Do you promise me that you won't do that?"

Her tone was so intense that it scared me. "I promise," I said.

"When you recapitulate, you are dissolving the relationship," Dianne explained. "Don't recapitulate anyone unless you are truly willing to let the relationship go. Once you do it, it is gone."

CHAPTER 12

Regaining My Power

DON JUAN'S GROUP of mystics teaches that a great deal of psychic energy is tied up in our relationships. I would have to agree.

I spent time each week recapitulating my previous romantic encounters, almost always walking to the circle of trees to do my ritual in their sacred presence. When it was the dead of winter and freezing cold, I simply bundled myself in long underwear and wool pants, sweaters, a coat, mittens, and a scarf and hat.

The recapitulation was a painstaking process, requiring me to call up every scene, every experience, with each person I had dated. I even recapitulated the conversations, gestures, thoughts and clothing of other people who were present in our shared moments. It took all my strength.

I saw that my vision was omniscient. Some part of me witnessed everything I did and everything I thought. It knew what I was doing, even when I did not. It even knew what was going on inside of the other people with whom I interacted. The Witness existed, just the way the yoga books described.

I saw that every unconscious thought and belief I had about myself played out in my relationships. I had repeated the same patterns again and again. No wonder I had the same types of experiences over and over.

I would not repeat these patterns again. My clear intent would keep me out of trouble, but also out of a real relationship for quite some time.

As I recapitulated, my previous boyfriends called me one by one. I ran into the first man I recapitulated at a party and arranged to get my scarf back. Even a college boyfriend, whom I had not spoken with in more than a dozen years, called me out of the blue from Europe, where he was now living, asking quite insistently to see me. It was uncanny.

Dianne explained that as I recapitulated, they could no longer suck energy from me. While it was a gain for me, it was a loss for them. They called because they wanted to hold on. They wanted to keep their power source.

At one point, I received an invitation to the art opening of a man with whom I had once been in love. He had continued to call me after we broke up, even when he was living with another woman, the one for whom he had left me. I somehow imagined he really loved me and would be back. Although I resisted his attentions, they prevented me from dating anyone else for several years. Until I did the Recapitulation, I couldn't see that he cared only for himself.

Curious, I went to the opening. When I saw him again, I couldn't imagine why I had ever been interested. It was as if I had become a different person.

A S I RECAPITULATED, I became more aware of other people's energies. I could sense what people were thinking and feeling. I noticed that I could feel and see people's sexual energies as well, especially if they were focused on me. I found that I could also see this energy in dogs, which I felt more comfortable studying.

This energy wasn't anything I could describe to anyone. I could just see it. This sexual energy, which had once been so mesmerizing, was now just energy. I had a detachment and awareness that I had never had before. I was becoming the master of these energies instead of their victim.

I had read in one of the yoga books that when an Enlightened Master initiates a person, the *kundalini shakti*, the spiritual energy, begins to purify all of the subtle energy centers located along the spine. I had the sense that the vortex at the pelvic region, the one that regulates sexual energy, was being purified. Rigorously.

CHAPTER 13

The Council of Light

I ALWAYS ASKED DIANNE what she did during our sessions. I liked to hear the mysterious details and Dianne was always happy to tell me. She never seemed to lose patience with me or get offended by my constant questions, or by my sarcasm and doubt, which I merely considered normal and natural.

But on one particular occasion, not long after we had started working together, Dianne seemed shaken. "Come sit down," she said, after she finished the energy work. I got off the table in her healing room and followed her back to her parlor.

"The Council of Light came," she said, rather slowly and solemnly, sitting up very straight. "They told me that you are a healer."

"Dianne, I can't even see an aura. That's just ridiculous," I protested. "I am not a healer. I could never do what you do."

The work Dianne did amazed and fascinated me. Perhaps I even longed to have gifts that could be used to help others. Still, I would never want to be that "woo-woo." What would my friends think? What about my magazine career? I wouldn't give that up. But somewhere deep inside, I longed to understand how healing energy worked. I felt it would give me a window into the secrets of the universe.

"You know," Dianne said, "only healers work as hard as you do at healing yourself. All I can tell you is that you are a healer. You are going to be known as a healer."

"Who is this Council of Light?" I asked suspiciously. I tended to think she was making stuff like this up when she mentioned masters from other dimensions. Yet she always acted as if she was simply reporting the facts.

"The Council is group of very high beings," she explained. She listed a few saintly figures with who I was completely unfamiliar. Then she mentioned Jesus Christ, for whom I felt a deep reverence.

"Jesus Christ?"

Despite my doubts about a Council, I was comforted to know that Jesus might be watching over me. Nevertheless, Dianne's assessment of my destiny frightened me. I just couldn't see how it could ever be that way. At that time, it seemed far more likely to me that I would become a bag lady.

Since losing my job at the *Journal*, I had almost no magazine assignments. Even the weekly Sunday magazine where I had been writing cover stories dropped me. My editor there seemed uncomfortable when I called. I imagined at an editorial meeting they had decided, "Let's not use Diane anymore," and that was it.

All of my friends and former colleagues were climbing the mastheads at their respective publications. I was sinking into oblivion. The idea that some "Council of Light" would visit me during a healing—or at any other time—seemed unfathomable.

Deciding she had probably said more than she should, especially considering my attitude, Dianne clammed up and refused to name any more names. Normally, that would have made me press harder for more information. But I was relieved. It was more than I could absorb.

"Well, I'll believe it when I see it," I told Dianne defiantly.

She shrugged. "Well, that's what *they* said." Apparently, in her view, it didn't matter what *I* thought, as if my own life wasn't actually up to me. What would be, would be.

CHAPTER 14

Visiting the Mother

"**D**O YOU WANT to go see Mother Meera?" Kim called to ask a few months after our dinner together. "I made reservations and now my friend can't come. You could take his place."

Her question took me completely by surprise. We hadn't talked since we had dinner. Plus, I didn't know one could go to see Mother Meera. But immediately, I wanted to go.

I told Kim if I could come up with the money for the plane fare, I'd go with her. It seemed unlikely. With my career on the skids, I found it increasingly difficult to call people I knew for assignments, or even just to say hello. It never turned out well, and only made me feel more hopeless. I had done so many cover stories and worked for so many top publications. But now it was as if there was an invisible force field blocking me. How did I become a *persona non grata*? What was to become of me? I didn't know. I felt I was dissolving.

Nevertheless, when I got off the phone with Kim, I called the editor of a yoga magazine to whom I had sent my clips a few weeks earlier. Within minutes I had an assignment to write a story about Mother Meera.

Kim and I committed to spending twelve days in the town where Mother Meera lived. On the Friday, Saturday, Sunday and Monday nights of two consecutive weekends, we would have *darshan*, an audience with Mother Meera. In the days in between, we would rest, relax, and walk around the little town and in the beautiful fields all around us.

Ingrid, who had brought me to meet the Teacher, stridently objected to this trip. "You already have a Teacher," she told me. Nevertheless, I felt pulled to go. I didn't think of myself as having a Teacher. Besides, if these people had any power, didn't they all work for the same "office?" I had a feeling if the Teacher was my Teacher, then this had her blessing. After all, there was that *force* again, stronger than any ocean tide I had ever felt, drawing me to Mother Meera.

IN THE EARLY evenings in the small town outside of Frankfurt, we lined up on a suburban street, waiting to enter the house where Mother Meera gave her audiences. These audiences with *The Mother*, as everyone called her, were in silence. They took place in what looked like a large suburban recreation room, complete with linoleum tile floors.

The Mother, a petite Indian woman who was nearly the same age as me, was quite beautiful. Each night she wore the most luminous saris, usually threaded with gold. When she came into the room, everyone rose to greet her and an electric energy lit up the place.

Once she sat down, the silent visits began as, one by one, we knelt before her on a silk cushion and took hold of her feet. She gently took each person's head in her hands and, barely touching, did a few motions with her fingers. With this brief ministration, *The Mother* was said to bring light to the soul. Then the person would look up into her eyes and by gazing back in to that person's eyes, *The Mother* would give some help to his or her personality and life circumstances. Then the audience would be over, and it would be the next person's turn. Each audience, or *darshan*, took perhaps a minute, but was said to have life-changing effects.

The silence of these evenings was mysterious and intoxicating. There were rows and rows of simple chairs. I, however, sat cross-legged on the floor, just a few feet from *The Mother*. If I could, I would have climbed into her lap, if it meant I would get an extra transfusion of help. Each night my forehead throbbed painfully, right where the "third eye" is said to be. I felt as if I had a unicorn's horn growing from my forehead. When I touched the spot, however, I couldn't feel anything there. Still, I could not release the intense pressure.

Despite these sensations and my longing for healing, I wondered if I was insane. I consoled myself with the notion that I was there as a journalist, observing. I didn't have to believe this woman had some kind of Divine power or light. If she did, well, then, that would be a bonus.

ALAS, THE ASSIGNMENT wasn't working out. At first, Mother Meera's secretary had said yes, I could have an interview with *The Mother*. I was elated. Then, the very next day the secretary said an interview wouldn't be possible; *The Mother* had changed her mind. I was distressed.

The secretary told me I could call during regular telephone hours, like any devotee of *The Mother*, anywhere in the world, and ask any questions that I wanted. I would not be turned away.

Dutifully, I walked into town late one afternoon and placed a call to *The Mother* from a pay phone. The secretary answered and spoke for *The Mother*, who was sitting nearby.

"What is this transformation of the world that you talk about?" I asked *The Mother*. The secretary relayed my question. I could hear *The Mother* speaking in the background, in her musical, lilting tones.

"It is a transformation in each individual," the secretary replied, translating for *The Mother*. "Don't you feel it?"

I didn't know what to say. I couldn't feel it. And it wasn't a very satisfying interview. Soon, the secretary told me it was time to get off the phone. Other people wanted to speak to *The Mother*.

When I went for *Darshan* that night, I burned with anger and distress.

Soon after I fell asleep that night, I woke from the most fantastic, disturbing dreams of my life. In the first one:

> *I was very proud of my latest celebrity interview, a magazine cover story. It was a good story, the kind until recently, I had been doing quite a bit. Celebrity profiles were easy to do, and paid relatively well. Plus I felt I received a glimmer of reflected stardust. Seeing my byline always made me feel I*

had done something, my voice counted. My existence and my value were confirmed. I was somebody.

But this time my editors had made a terrible mistake. The story came out with someone else's byline on it. To underscore the problem, one of my brashest journalist friends, Dennis, called to taunt me. "What's the matter?" he said. "What happened to your byline?"

I woke in a cold sweat. The energy of the dream was that of a hair-raising nightmare, for in it I had somehow been erased, as if I didn't really exist. As I sat up in bed contemplating it, the message became clear: As a writer, I had to focus on the content of what I was writing, not my byline and status. In my ordinary, waking life I had only received kudos for these stories. Yet I sensed there might not be any glib celebrity profiles in my future. All in all, it was an angry rap on the knuckles. It was confusing because I didn't think I had done anything wrong.

Eventually I calmed down and fell back to sleep. Soon I had a second, more horrifying dream:

Someone had gotten murdered. I couldn't discern or retain any details but the annihilation was terrible and absolute.

I woke up drenched in sweat, shaking. In a flash, more of the dream came to the surface: I knew that *the person who had been murdered was me.*

Still shaking, I turned on the light. The meaning of the dream came immediately: *I, my ego, was going to be killed. There would be no escape. It would be done.*

I glanced around the simple little room of the modest B&B. The cheery white curtains framing the window seemed reassuring. But I knew nothing on God's earth could protect me from my fate. From a spiritual perspective this "murder," or death, of the ego might be considered a good thing. Still I didn't want to stick around for it. I sensed, however, that I would have no choice.

The second dream was a sequel to the first. It seemed I wouldn't be writing to satisfy my ego much longer. Success could no longer be a driving force. I couldn't imagine what I would be doing instead.

And to think: this experience had unfolded from a healing in which Goddesses had come to visit, a healing that had left me smirking in disbelief.

By the time I arrived for my final *darshan*, I was in a terrible state. *What would become of me? What kind of Mother was she?*

As I kneeled before her, the answer came. I heard it within my own being, yet I knew the message came from the Mother: *You are not here as a journalist, but as a seeker. You cannot hide behind your career.*

WHEN OUR STAY was over, Kim and I took a ride back to the Frankfurt airport in a car with some other people who had been seeing *The Mother*. It was a warm day in June. All of a sudden, on the autobahn I saw a few flakes of snow outside the windshield. *Was I having a vision?* I wondered. *Or seeing a mirage?*

I realized everyone in the car was seeing the same thing. We were transfixed. And then the flakes were gone. *Maybe it was embers of some kind?* Yet it definitely had looked like snow. I couldn't explain it. Neither could Kim or anyone else in the car. We drove in a hushed silence.

Had the trip been a waste? Was anything different? I asked myself as I landed back at JFK International Airport in NYC. After getting my luggage, I waited on line for a taxi. When my turn finally came, a voice in my head said: *Let this one go by. Don't get in.*

I had waited a long time. Why would I give up a taxi to someone else? But mostly I was worried about being rude and snubbing the driver. As soon as I got in I noticed the taxi had an awful, stale smell. *You can still get out,* the voice in my head implored. I ignored it, afraid to seem strange or rude.

As we drove out of the terminal and away from the safety of other people and the help they could provide, I realized the driver had a surly demeanor, more unpleasant than the sour odor of his vehicle. *It's his surliness that you are smelling*, the voice told me. *That's why it is so foul in here*. In a way this voice was very familiar to me. It had always been there. But it had never seemed so dominant. Besides, I had had many years of practice in ignoring and overriding it.

The driver suggested a roundabout route into NYC that would have doubled my fare. I insisted that we take the 495 Expressway. It was the most direct route. Plus, the dramatic view it afforded of the skyline always gave me a rush and reminded me that I had arrived home. The driver complied. I relaxed.

Then we hit traffic. The driver turned around, yelling and cursing, accusing me of ruining his day and destroying his life. His words and demeanor were frighteningly violent. *This is why you weren't supposed to get in this car*, the voice explained.

"What do you want me to do now?" The driver finally screamed at me with satanic rage.

"I want you to turn around and drive the taxi," I said in a normal voice, as if we were having a reasonable conversation.

He seemed as surprised by my firmness as I. He complied, yet I could still feel him seething.

When we got to my apartment, I got out, got my bags and paid my fare. Because of his abuse I decided not to tip. He came after me, screaming, menacing. My doorman escorted me into the building. *Thank God I have a doorman. I could have been in real trouble. Next time, I better pay attention to my inner guidance.*

No one had explained it to me, but I knew that that voice I heard in my head at the taxi stand was my higher Self, the inner Teacher.

I vaguely sensed that this heightened perception was a gift from *The Mother*.

A Magical Place

I WENT FOR a weekend at the Teacher's retreat center soon after returning from *The Mother*. The story I told myself was that it would be a good way to take a little vacation without spending too much money. It was true that in those days you could go stay at the Teacher's school for quite a modest fee. You merely had to stay in a big dorm room with many people, or in a small room where eight people shared a bathroom and four bunk beds.

Something besides a budget vacation must have been driving me. I just couldn't admit it to myself. I was certainly not the type of person to visit an ashram, or share a room with a stranger, let alone with dozens of other people. Yet that is what I did.

I found, against all logic, that the big dormitory was my favorite place for sleeping in the ashram. It was a silent dorm. That meant no one spoke once inside the dorm. Although there were over one hundred beds, it was very quiet, muffled by velvet, not only velvet drapes, but velvet energy.

I felt totally safe. No one ever rifled through any of my belongings or took so much as a capful of my shampoo. The safeness I felt was also on a much deeper level, as if I was in a place where I was protected.

Nevertheless I watched for signs that it was a cult. I brought my books and my journal and kept to myself. I was oblivious of the ashram schedule, except when it came to meals. I wondered how other people there knew each other and could be so friendly. Although I wanted to keep my distance, I also felt a little left out. Hardly any one spoke to me. Certainly, I was not the target of any recruitment. That eased my concerns.

On that first summer visit I noticed how beautiful the grounds were. There were lawns to sit on and flowers decorating the walkways. A wooded area gave way to a lake you could walk around for contemplation and reflection. The place radiated a magical peace and beauty.

A path for contemplation also ran through the woods, connecting one area of the center to another. Once, as I walked along that path, I ran into one of the swamis. She flashed me a smile of such delight and recognition that I have never forgotten that moment. It was a smile of pure love.

Everything about the ashram seemed serene and mysteriously healing. The Temple was stunning. It housed a *murti*, a statue of the grandfather of the lineage. It was said to be enlivened by Brahmin priests with *prana*, or spiritual energy. There were always beautiful fresh flowers decorating the altar, chosen not only for their dramatic, deep, pure colors, but also for their delicious, sweet scents, which perfumed the air and intoxicated the soul.

On subsequent visits, I found the place to be just as peaceful and comforting. I was left completely to myself. I sat in the meditation cave every day for long meditation sessions. As I began to offer service and do chores, I started to meet people and feel more at home.

Sometimes I went to the early evening or the early morning chant. I found the chants soothing. Besides, it was the thing to do, sort of like going to happy hour if you were on a cruise. Some part of me was very drawn to these activities, but I couldn't quite accept it yet.

My interest in chanting increased after one particular evening chant, which was always introduced with a long solo from a huge drum. The insistent, methodical and mysterious beat built up a strange longing and excitement in me, and went directly into my heart. The drum roll gave way when the singing began.

I read the words of the chant from a laminated sheet with the Sanskrit transliterated into English letters to aide pronunciation. As I held it, I realized the page was subtly vibrating. *Was it my hands?* I watched carefully to see. *No, it was not my hands. It was the vibration of the chant, from everyone chanting at the same time.* I realized that same vibration was going into me, affecting all of my cells.

I had been given a visceral glimpse of the power of prayer.

CHAPTER 16

Old Friends,
New Perceptions

I WENT TO SEE a good friend who had cracked her jaw biting into a peach pit. Instead of healing, her jaw bone was dissolving. Her doctors wired her jaw shut to help it heal. Seeing her plight, I felt she needed some other kind of medicine. I urged her to see a healer. She was incensed. She wrote what she thought in a little note, and handed it to me. "How dare you suggest such a thing," her note said.

That turned out to be the last time I saw this friend. I still loved and respected her. We just couldn't be friends any more. I had changed. I no longer fitted into my old life, any more than I could wear a favorite sweater after it shrank in the dryer.

I didn't understand that my resonance was changing. Nor could I yet comprehend that since everything in the outer world is a manifestation of one's magnetic resonance, my life had to change. It wasn't just my inner state that was getting rearranged, but also my outer relationships. It was frightening. It made me wonder if I was losing my sanity. It was as if I had stepped into *The Twilight Zone* and couldn't get back.

Yet the more aspects of my life dissolved, the more I gained. Sometimes, for instance, when I got on the subway after a healing session the people I saw mesmerized me. The most "ordinary" people were exquisitely radiant. These were people who had spent the day working. Their faces might be tired. They might look dragged down. The dingy light and grunge of the subway made it all seem worse. Yet I could see the light in them, and around them. Sometimes the intoxication and beauty was so intense I felt like crying. *"You're high, Goldner,"* I'd tell myself. *"Get a grip. It's from the healing."* It was true that after healings this type of experience became quite normal. But it was also happening at other times.

Even when I turned on the television it was as if new dimensions had opened up. Instead of just seeing the flat surface, I could see beneath to a truer reality. When I watched *Larry King Live* I wanted to know: *What kind of soul does his guest have?* It was hard to stare at people face to face, but I could look at people's souls on television to my heart's content.

One night I watched King interview a particularly powerful politician. At first, my heart contracted in response to what I perceived as his arrogance. Then I saw that underneath, at a level where he might not even be aware, he felt small and lonely. I experienced an overwhelming wave of compassion and wished I could help this man release the pain in his heart. Meanwhile, when a guest on the show was open-hearted, Larry King began to glow.

The rest of my life was in tatters. But this type of experience was completely enthralling. I sat in front of the television transfixed. All I had to do was tune in and I could see a plane of existence that was much deeper and truer than the reality I once knew.

CHAPTER 17

Recapitulation: Further Adventures

EVEN THOUGH I had seen the effects of the Recapitulation, I still didn't realize quite how powerful it actually was, until I had a few more rather extraordinary experiences.

One day, I decided to recapitulate some themes that threaded through my life. In this approach, I allowed my inner guidance to call up the appropriate scenes. Before long, an incident with my mother popped up. I began recapitulating it. I didn't think a few minutes of recapitulation could matter much, considering the length and intensity of the relationship. Besides, I was recapitulating a theme, not my relationship with my mother.

I had barely finished the exercise when my mother called. "Are you okay?" she asked, sounding frantic, as if she had heard that I had died.

I never recapitulated anything having to do with either of my parents again.

Instead, I turned my attention to a girl who had been a good friend. Gayle had grown up in a wealthy and well-connected family on a sprawling estate outside of Manhattan. It was a very different background than I had, growing up in the modest environs of Bayside, Queens. Like me, however, Gayle was in the magazine business and we lived just a few blocks from each other. We got together often, and often spontaneously.

I treasured Gayle's companionship, our easy friendship, and our mutual interest in the business. But Gayle was the kind of person who seemed to become an even better friend when I was writing the *Daily News* society page, or when a best-selling novelist began to squire me around town. When I broke off the novelist's attentions, my stock dipped. She didn't call as often to get updates from me or invite me to as many of her parties. By then, so much of my life was dissolving that perhaps she didn't know what to do with me.

It was an incident that had happened several years earlier that prompted my recapitulation. At a party Gayle hosted, one of her junior editors congratulated me on a story I wrote for another magazine. "The editor says you are such a good writer," the girl gushed. "You must start writing for us." I realized that Gayle was standing behind me, signaling for the girl to stop what she was saying. Gayle didn't want me to write for her magazine.

I am sure Gayle had her reasons. But I had never dealt with this incident. Now I wanted my power back. I no longer cared if that meant I would be alone or lonely or dirt poor.

After I had done some recapitulation, Gayle called me and asked me to brunch. My intention was to let her know that our friendship would have to change for the better. I didn't necessarily want to sever our tie.

We met at a sweet little place in the Village. Just when the people at the table right next to us left, and things seem to quiet down enough for the serious talk I planned, Gayle reached for the check. "I've got to be getting to the office," she said. That was the grand finale of our friendship. I knew that there was no point in trying to establish further contact. My only connection to Gayle after that was when I read about her career moves or her engagement and marriage in the newspapers. Recapitulation was serious business.

CHAPTER 18

Falling Apart

U NTIL I MET the Teacher, I had little awareness that my
self-worth was the result of what I did, of whom I knew,
of outer things that could, apparently, change with the
wind.

I had been swept along by my ambitions and friend-
ships, my anxieties and dreams, my interest in literature and writing. I
had never questioned the foundation of my life, the many assumptions
I had about how things worked, who I was, my purpose, or the goals I
had set for myself.

Now all my moorings were gone, my career, my friends, the way
I spent my time, my basic beliefs about how "reality" worked. My
self-esteem melted away, or rather, I discovered that it had never
really existed. Plus, my anxiety was overwhelming. It seemed that all my
very worst nightmares, the kind of secret fears that many people harbor, had
suddenly become manifest, and all at the same time. The same way I could
suddenly see the truer reality as I looked at others, I could see myself.

The Teacher once told a group of us that were gathered with her,
that before she can help anyone transform, she first has to show us
what's wrong. But that was years later. At the time I began dissolving, I
didn't have any framework for the drastic unraveling I was experiencing. My psyche was being spiritually sandblasted, washing away eons

of grime and debris.

Anxiety had always shadowed me. At the beginning of my last semester of college, I was paralyzed when faced with choosing my final set of classes. I vowed then that I would consider my life a success if I could only become calm and clear.

Now my anxiety was unbearable and constant. It was as if I could suddenly experience my emotional state in ten dimensions instead of the usual two or three. It was a searing of my soul that I wasn't sure, at times, that I would survive.

This intensity and depth of awareness, I would slowly come to understand, was one result of the awakening initiated by the Teacher. I didn't have an inkling of what I had gotten myself into it, or how the process worked. But somehow a blindingly radiant light had been lit inside and was shining on everything in my life. I had no idea that what was occurring might actually be beneficial, a dissolving out of things that I didn't need, that weren't helpful. Looking back, I can say it was the best thing that ever happened to me. But at the time, I feared that I wouldn't make it. I felt I was holding on to the edge of a cliff and couldn't claw my way back up to firm ground.

At first, a healing only seemed to make my anxiety worse. Then, after a week or so, the anxiety would not only subside, but my state would be better than ever, as if something had purified out of me. It never ceased to be miraculous. I slowly learned that when you add light, whatever is obscuring the light must come up and be resolved.

Whatever I worked on in healing sessions increased my illumination. The new perspective shifted everything, from how I responded to things, to what experiences I would draw to me. If I worked on anxiety, my anxiety would spike and then be less intense than before. Likewise, if I had a healing where I worked on speaking up, I would find myself in a situation where I suddenly had to speak up in a new way. If a healing put light on my relationships, I would see other people more clearly.

I woke up the morning after one healing and could hardly get out of bed. My muscles had stiffened so much I was almost in a state of *rigor mortis*. Dianne had put light on some relationship dynamics in my life. "You are afraid to let the information in," she told me. I literally had stiffened every muscle in my body against the awareness rising to the surface of my consciousness.

Finally, the knowledge I needed filtered into my awareness. At first it rattled me. After a few weeks it no longer seemed so terrible and I found a new steadiness within.

I was experiencing a level of transformation beyond anything I could have imagined. Inspired, I sent one of my girlfriends for a healing after she lost her job at a publishing house. After a few sessions, she got an even better position with a different company. I was happy for her, yet the contrast to my situation was almost unbearable. Why couldn't that new job happen for me?

"Because of the work you will be doing later," Dianne said. "Because of the number of people you will be helping."

SEEING INTO THE SPIRIT REALMS

CHAPTER 19

Seeing

"WHAT DO YOU see?" I asked each healer I met. Gerda turned my question around. "What do you see?"

"Me?" I replied. "Nothing."

"That's not true," Gerda said. "You see."

"No, I don't," I said, surprised by her firmness.

"Just give it a try," Gerda insisted. We were in a hotel on Long Island, where the Barbara Brennan School of Healing was in session, drinking juice with several of Gerda's classmates late in the evening. Gerda, I quickly learned, would always demand more from me than I thought I had.

"Look at her knee," she insisted, gesturing to a woman in our group who was wearing a big clunky leg brace. "Tell me what you see."

Instinctively, I closed my eyes. I didn't see anything except this gray light in my mind's eye. "Gray?" I said.

"That's right," Gerda said. She turned my attention towards the next person at the table. "Just close your eyes and tell me the first thing about her that pops into your mind."

I saw a grid of white light in the person's chest. "I don't see anything," I said, sure that I was imagining it.

"Just tell me what you see," Gerda repeated. So I described the grid.

"Yes!" she said. "You're right."

Soon Gerda taught me to see the matrix of energy that exists around each person. We didn't have to be sitting with them. The person could be anywhere in the world when I did the scan. "What does Joe's grid look like?" Gerda asked one day.

"Well, I see a tangle," I said, hesitantly.

"That's right," Gerda confirmed.

"Now look at the grid for Sally," she instructed.

Trying to see the subtle levels made everything go blank. I closed my eyes and waited for the image to come to me. Sally's matrix appeared on my inner mind screen. "It's basically very neat and orderly," I reported. "But there's some darkness at the center, well camouflaged."

Gerda was pleased.

Gerda made seeing clairvoyantly so easy. I realized this seeing had always been there. It's just that no one had ever asked me to look. It was often subtle, like a whisper, and easy to miss, unless you paid attention. Yet it was a deeper, truer level of reality. When I tried to force or grab the information; it would dissolve. All I could do was surrender and allow whatever was there to show itself to me. Then the information would simply be there.

Gerda also encouraged me to read people's energy fields, even at a distance. I learned, in particular, to tune into the energy vortexes along the spine. These vortexes bring in energy and information from outside and regulate the flow of energy and consciousness inside each person. Each vortex is responsible for modulating specific emotional, physical and spiritual aspects of a person's life. When I could see how a particular vortex or chakra was flowing, I could tell a great deal about that person's physical, emotional and spiritual issues and tendencies.

For instance, if the energy was congealed at the throat center, as it was with me, a person might have difficulty speaking up or in manifesting their dreams. On a physical level, they might be susceptible to problems with their thyroid or have other problems related to the throat or speaking. A person whose energy isn't flowing in the pelvic area might have trouble processing emotions and have intestinal issues. Women might have problems related to their monthly cycle or their fertility.

When I looked at people's energy fields, I didn't see colors. Instead, I had a sense of where there was more or less light, where energy was congealed, and where energy was open and flowing.

ALTHOUGH I COULD see clairvoyantly, somehow this vision wasn't always with my eyes. It was more of a knowing. Yet every so often I would see the light with my physical eyes, too. Once I was in the lobby of a hotel and when I looked at a group of people standing there, I noticed sparkles of light around my friend Thomas. I knew it was because he meditated a lot. It was breathtaking to see so much radiant light around him. I also saw the light around Gerda; it was very clear, bright and sharp, like Gerda herself.

Another time, Gerda and I were on the phone. "What's that dark spot on the ceiling?" she suddenly asked.

"There's no spot on the ceiling."

Gerda insisted. "Yes, there is," she said.

"No," I said. "There isn't anything on the ceiling." As I spoke, I watched a moth sitting high up on a wall, out of reach. Finally, I mentioned the moth, resting on the wall just below the ceiling.

"Oh, that's what it is," she said. Gerda did not like moths. "That's a dark energy someone sent you," she said. "Hold on." She got quiet as she transmitted. All of a sudden there was a very bright, clear light around the moth, almost like a spotlight. There was nothing subtle about this light. I knew it was the light Gerda had trained on it from her home in Virginia.

"Okay," Gerda said after a few minutes. "You can get a paper cup and take it outside." Without putting up a fight, the moth went into the cup and when I opened the window, it flew away.

THERE WERE MANY uses for seeing clairvoyantly. I learned one great tool from Catherine Karas, another healer who had studied with Barbara Brennan.

At the time, I had been working on my book proposal for more than a year. When my agent submitted it, every single publisher rejected it. Some of the rejections were lovely. One editor even asked if I would ghost write someone else's book. But I wanted to write my book. I decided the solution would be to sign with a new, more powerful agent. I had narrowed my decision down to two agents, but couldn't figure out which one to go with.

"That's easy," Catherine said. "Just see which one has more light."

"That's easy for you to say," I said.

"You can do it. Just close your eyes and call each of them up as light," advised Catherine.

I closed my eyes and imagined two spheres of light, the one on the right representing agent A, and the one on the left, agent B.

"Is one brighter?" she asked.

One of the two agents definitely had a brighter glow.

"That's your agent," she said.

She turned out to be right. I soon had a terrific agent.

Seeing clairvoyantly was a very useful skill indeed.

CHAPTER 20

Spirit Guides

I
T WAS VERY hard for me to believe that spiritual guides might actually exist. Though the idea intrigued me, it also terrified me. It was the ultimate forbidden zone. I had been raised to believe that spirits simply didn't exist. The only things you could believe in were what scientists could quantify.

Of course, accepting the idea of subtle energy had been challenging at first. Yet once I began to see and feel the energy, I simply couldn't deny the reality of it. I'd be a coward. Besides, I came to believe, from the scientific research done in this area, that subtle energy was no more or less metaphysical than electricity or sub-atomic particles.

But spirit guides? Angels? Ascended masters? Could one ever prove such beings existed? I had never seen them. If I could see them, then I might accept them. And, if I did see them, it would turn my world upside down and inside out. Would it mean that God existed? Would it be proof of higher spiritual realms? I just couldn't go there. It was a boundary line I refused to cross.

I tolerated the references to spirit guides from healers, including Dianne, because that's the way they talked. I couldn't change that. But I couldn't help but wonder sometimes if they were making up the visitations and visions they described.

Then one day I had the surprise of my life.

In those days, I couldn't go to sleep before one or two in the morning, sometimes even later. Waking at 8 a.m. or even as late as 9 a.m. I felt like a sloth. I asked Dianne to do a shamanic journey to help me become an early riser.

As I lay on her healing table, I could hear her call in spirit guides. The next morning at five o'clock, I was wide-eyed. I felt as if something or someone had awakened me. *Who? Or what?*

As I lay in bed, I became aware of the sound of drumming and rattles being shaken practically in my ear. It was faint, as if I was hearing something in another room or, in this case, another dimension. It felt as if a tribe of medicine men was dancing around me. I could feel the faintest flutter in the air. *Had I gone over the edge?*

I got very still. Yes, I could hear drumming and rattles. I couldn't see the medicine men. But they were making quite a racket. *A whole tribe of spirit guides. Drumming just for me.* I was shocked. I was also tired. I rolled over and went back to sleep.

The medicine men came back for several mornings at five o'clock. Each morning, exhausted, I rolled over and went back to sleep. Finally, they gave up on me. I missed them at first. I had a lingering sense of failure. I learned then that a person's will trumps everything: healing energy, angels, masters and spirit guides. If you don't want to do something, no spiritual being is going to make you do it, even if it's the best thing for you.

It took several years before I managed to become an early riser, something I associated with being productive and focused in life. Nevertheless my encounter with the medicine men from another dimension was a mind-opening experience. I now knew that spiritual beings exist. It was a little like realizing the world is round when everyone else still thinks it is flat. I vowed that I wouldn't mention my little secret to anyone.

The only way I could square this new reality was to accept that life exists in a range of dimensions or frequencies, just the way life exists in a range of sizes from the microscopic to elephantine. It's hard for people to believe in higher beings if they can't see them. Indeed, most people couldn't accept the idea of germs, either—until someone invented the microscope.

The medicine men were the proof to me that the higher planes exist.

I would have many more encounters with spirits, angels and ascended masters as time went on. Indeed, visits from higher beings would become a part of life for me.

CHAPTER 21

A Power Animal

"ICALL ON OWL," I heard Dianne say. I was so deep into myself on the healing table that I felt as if I was dreaming her voice, except that it became more urgent, as if someone was in danger, as if Dianne was afraid I was flying away. I heard her call in a raptor, a bird of prey.

My eyes were closed and the room was dark. Yet immediately, I could see the magnificent creature with my inner eye, on what you could call my mind screen. It was huge and fierce, with sharp talons and glinting eyes, smack in front of my face.

Dianne always seemed to have doe-like energy, very gentle and sweet. This raptor had a much more fierce energy. I had no idea Dianne had that kind of power. I made a mental note not to get on her bad side.

A few days later, I took one of my long walks along the East River, contemplating my life, praying for help. Suddenly I saw the raptor out over the water. It was like a hologram projected over the water against the sky, as if the boundaries between dimensions had dissolved. I looked away sure that I was imagining it, but when I looked again it was still there. It flew along with me for a while as I walked. It seemed very real to me. Yet I sensed that if I pointed it out to a friend, they would not be able to see it.

I called Dianne as soon as I got home. "I saw your power animal, the bird of prey," I reported. "Why is it hanging around me?"

"That's not my power animal," said Dianne. "It must be yours."

"Mine? That couldn't be mine. You called on it in the healing," I protested.

"Yes, but it's not my power animal."

That fierce creature was *my* power animal?

IN THE NATIVE American tradition, each animal has different medicine or power, based on its nature. Animal spirits bring these powers to their human companions, serving as a teacher and guide.

A few years earlier I had a few sessions with a metaphysically oriented therapist. She suggested that I try a session with a woman who retrieved power animals; it would help to empower me.

During this session, the animal spirit that stepped forward was a wolf. Because of his hunting prowess, he could call a taxi for me or find things I had misplaced. It sounded outlandish. Still, I asked my Wolf "friend" for help here and there.

I was instructed to say with any request: "If it is for the best of all possible things. That or something better." There was always a caveat, a reason why a request should not be fulfilled when it didn't manifest—it was not for the best. I was never sure about the whole thing.

This raptor was another story. I could see it.

A minute after I hung up from Dianne, I called her back. "What exactly are power animals, anyway?"

"They are from the fifth dimension," she said.

"What is the fifth dimension?" I asked.

"They're beyond time and space," she explained.

"What does that mean?'

"That's all I can tell you." She changed the direction of the conversation, explaining how to care for my power animal. I could "feed" it by dancing its dance or singing it a song that I made up. I could also call on the power animal for help.

My raptor, she explained, had vision, flew to great heights and could help me see the big picture. The raptor was also a fierce hunter and could give me strength and wisdom. The relationship between a person and a power animal is a sacred partnership. I could feed it love, sing the power animal its song, and give it experiences in this dimension, and the power animal would be my teacher and guide.

I would have thought the power animal was some kind of metaphor, except that I had seen it. When no one could see or hear me, in the shower, and sometimes by the East River, I sang to my raptor. I gave it power. I figured it couldn't hurt.

The power animal must have liked my songs. It came to me again and again. In those days, I was very myopic, literally and on other levels as well, though I didn't understand how blind I was. My raptor offered me its power of vision.

CHAPTER 22

A Prophetic Vision

SOON AFTER DISCOVERING my power animal, I went on a job interview for a new afternoon daily paper. With its limited resources, and even more limited cache, it represented a further fall in my fortunes. But I liked the editor, who had years of experience at an established New York paper. Besides, I needed to earn some money. When the editor took out a talisman from his pocket that he had been given by Mother Teresa, I took it as a sign and accepted the position.

The editor telephoned a day later to tell me that I would have to meet with the owner before the offer could be finalized. He apologized for the mix-up. Before I knew it, I found myself in the new owner's office, chatting about the newspaper business, about which he clearly knew very little. He had made his money through a series of financial deals.

When the financier picked up a phone call, I inwardly asked for guidance about the job. I had no idea what, if any, answer would emerge. I did most of this type of inward asking almost as a science project, just to see what would happen.

Almost immediately, to my amazement, my raptor flew in through a "window" behind the financier. The window didn't actually exist. But it was there in the "dream time" of the vision. The raptor did a back flip behind the owner and circled the room. Then, with a strange twist of its body, it flew out the "window." Then the window itself dissolved, as if it had never been there.

The owner chatted away, completely oblivious to the winged drama taking place. Even if I had pointed it out, I am sure he wouldn't have seen it. The whole thing seemed like a bizarre movie that unfolded in a timeless moment. By the clock it probably lasted no more than a minute.

What did it mean?

I found out soon enough. When the owner got off the phone, he insisted on hiring me as a writer, although I had been hired to be the features editor. That was the back flip.

A few weeks after I started the job, the financier fired the editor and the deputy editor. I saw that the financier was "twisted" when it came to owning a newspaper. Although I could have used the money, I gave my notice. The whole venture went down the tubes soon afterwards. What struck me as noteworthy was that many of the people on the small staff had a higher spiritual focus. Perhaps it was never about building a new newspaper, so much as providing a refuge for spiritually seeking souls needing a temporary respite.

M Y POWER ANIMAL showed up at the most surprising moments. For instance, I had a date with someone who had many attributes I was looking for in a partner. Instead of feeling excited, I felt anxiety and dread. I couldn't put my finger on why.

During a healing session Dianne asked me to call in my power animal to gain clarity about this date. "What do you see?" she asked.

My power animal circled high overhead while I saw myself swimming in the ocean with this man, who, like me, loved to swim. We were completely separate. The scene was barren and sterile and lonely.

"Well, you have your answer," Dianne said.

Another time, I ruminated on my life as I walked towards the farmers market in Union Square. It was a bright, sunny, winter day yet I was in the darkest place. Everything I used to do, and all of the people I knew, had simply fallen away.

My girlfriends and I no long got together. Like someone who loses their friends when they quit drinking, I couldn't discuss men with them because

I no longer felt like a hapless victim. We couldn't talk about the magazine business because I had become adrift from it. Plus I no longer went shopping, since I didn't need new outfits to meditate, nor did I have the money for such a pastime. I might as well have been living in a Himalayan cave instead of Manhattan.

Why couldn't I catch a break? I wondered. *Had I just screwed up my life irrevocably? Or was I going through a spiritual purification, a dark night of the soul?* At that very moment I asked the question, I got the answer as a truck went by on a cross street. On the side panel facing me, in huge letters, was a message from the raptor. It said: "Eagle Demolition."

The whole world was vibrating in some kind of amazing communion with me. It was as if, in some mystical way, I was completely interconnected with everything around me.

Because of these experiences, I signed up for a workshop on basic shamanism with Michael Harner, Ph.D., who launched The Foundation for Shamanic Studies and authored *The Way of the Shaman*. Harner was a shaman who had traveled the globe and worked with shamans from every tradition from Mongolia to Alaska to the Amazon. He had delved into the mysteries of the universe with some of the most powerful shamans alive on the planet. Yet clearly he enjoyed teaching beginners. I was lucky to train with such a master. He transmitted his love of shamanism and its power and its practicality.

Harner taught us how to slip into a deeply altered state just by listening to a drumbeat. By the end of the weekend, I could journey to the upper, lower and middle worlds to retrieve lost soul parts and also to find people's power animals. I could travel to these realms with my power animal to receive guidance for myself and others. We learned how to dance our animals and sing their songs and let go of any inhibitions we might have about communing with the spirit world in this dramatic, celebratory way. I also learned how to use "ordinary" garden rocks for divination.

What intrigued me the most was how much shamanism had in common with other healing modalities. I was beginning to see that there is a universal type of experience on the inner planes.

CHAPTER 23

The ABCs of
Subtle Energy

"**P**LACE YOUR HAND on the thigh of the person across from you, " Michael Mamas instructed. "Feel the skin, now the muscle, and now go deeper and feel the bone."

I was visiting Mamas' healing school in San Diego, as a guest participant. Mamas, who originally trained as a veterinarian, had been a teacher at the Brennan School before launching his own school. Being a veterinarian had been good training for Mamas. Long before he became a healer, he had learned to "feel" into animals to learn what was wrong with them.

As I sank through the layers of flesh on the thigh of the woman across from me, I was amazed by how spongy it felt. When you looked at her, she looked soft. But it was striking how much her thigh felt that way. I was definitely feeling more than flesh. I was feeling some kind of essence.

"Now," Michael instructed, "Everyone in the left row of chairs, please get up and move one seat." When the line of people had moved, I placed my hand on the thigh of the new person opposite me, and this time I felt a very taunt sinewy flesh. The thigh belonged to a woman who was lean and muscular. Her flesh felt much as she looked.

Michael had us feel the thighs of several more people. Each time, I felt a person's thigh, the flesh felt unique and different from all of the others.

Michael was making sure we got the message: People's bodies and their energy are related. You could feel into people. You could literally feel their muscles, nerves and bones with your hands, and their energy.

"You're feeling subtle energy all of the time," Michael told me when we talked afterwards.

"What do you mean?" I asked. Other healers had told me the same thing. One healer even pointed out how, when he shifted into a different state of consciousness, my whole body reacted. I could see his point. But my response had been primal. I wouldn't have even noticed it, if he hadn't pointed it out. All in all, I was pretty sure I didn't feel energy ever.

"Close your eyes," Michael suggested. I sat up in my chair and closed my eyes.

"Now imagine that you have just walked into a bar where you have been in the past. What do you feel? What do you sense?"

He waited for me to tune in. I could feel a heaviness. My throat closed up a bit from the smoke and darkness hanging in the air. The feeling was oppressive.

"Now let that image go. Imagine that you are walking into a church where you have been. What do you feel?"

The contrast was so dramatic I could hardly believe it. The church felt light and expansive. The soaring ceiling gave me a feeling of openness and possibility. I felt calm and uplifted.

"You just felt subtle energy," Michael said. "See, you've been doing it your whole life without realizing it."

The exercise was illuminating. Energy wasn't just in the body. It was everywhere, and in everything. *So what exactly was it?*

I LEARNED BY EXPERIENCE. Once, I had an earache that didn't respond to two sets of antibiotics. "What are you refusing to hear?" my friend Gerda asked.

"Nothing," I said, annoyed by the implication.

"There's something," she insisted.

Finally, I sat down to meditate. I asked inwardly if there was anything I needed to hear. Much to my surprise, I received an answer. I had been avoiding an inner message. It was about some minor detail in my life, not some cataclysmic epiphany. Yet, if I needed proof that no detail is too small to be important, as soon as I followed the guidance, my problem resolved. My doctor prescribed a third antibiotic and it worked immediately. Was it the antibiotic? Or, was it the fact that I had listened to my inner Self?

Another time, I had a recurring bladder infection. After several rounds of antibiotics, my friend Nancy, who is both a medical doctor and a practicing healer, told me, "You must figure out what is pissing you off." Although it annoyed me, I followed her guidance. In meditation I saw that something was "pissing" me off in a relationship. I dealt with it and I never had another bladder infection.

I was getting a tutorial on body symbology. Almost always there are deeper emotional, mental or spiritual issues underlying the physical. When the energy is released, the physical can shift as well. Over time I came to learn that when there is pain or disease, the body is almost always speaking for the soul, acting as a messenger.

As I healed various challenges of my own, I came to see that subtle energy is consciousness. My thoughts, feelings, beliefs, intentions, and my spiritual light were all aspects of my subtle energy. This energy, this consciousness, then forms the template for the body and also for future experiences. I began to see that understanding the subtle energies could be critical in many situations. And everything and everyone in the world has a subtle energy template.

CHAPTER 24

Transmitting Energy

OW DID HEALERS "send" energy? How did they transmute difficult energies? It's a question that I asked all the time. At first the answers didn't make sense to me. I almost felt that the healers were holding out on me. One evening, for instance, I had a headache. A friend who was a healer, without even laying hands on me, transmitted healing energy while we were in the same room. My headache dissolved. "How did you do that?" I asked, completely mystified.

"I don't know," he replied. "I just did it."

"But how?"

"I imagined your headache as a cloud and I dispersed it with light."

"But how?"

He shrugged. He couldn't really say any more.

That kind of answer drove me nuts.

The other answers I got seemed equally vague. "It's all about love," some healers told me.

"It's about intention," added others. One healer, who had been a forensic accountant, had a very practical mind. Fortunately, he was able to help me glimpse what he meant. "Everything we do starts with an intention," he told me. "If you want to lift your arm, you first have to have an intention to lift it. All energy follows intention. You move energy through intent."

Still other healers, like Barbara Brennan herself, talked about resonance. Simply by holding a vibration for harmony, a state of health and flow, one could invite another person to hold that vibration as well.

These answers seemed vague—until I started doing healings. At a workshop at a retreat center in upstate New York, Cheryl Ann, a woman I had met while interviewing healers and students at the Barbara Brennan School of Healing, sought me out as her partner. She was a very kind and patient woman who had no doubt I could do a healing and offered herself up as an early guinea pig. If it hadn't been for her, I probably would have sat on the sidelines that weekend, and maybe every weekend workshop after that.

Cheryl Ann told me not to worry about what was happening, just to have faith. She gave me her intention and I set to work. I ran energy through each of her chakras, as I had learned to do, and then I worked on running light into her busted knee. I repeated my mantra because I knew that was a high vibration. I intended for that energy to somehow go into her knee as I held my hands on it.

After a little while, I noticed a vibration between my hands and her knee. At first, I wondered if I was imagining it, but it was definitely there. As I kept intending light to go into her knee, the vibration got stronger and stronger. I knew that the healing light was somehow entering her. I was thrilled. It was as if I had, by intention, created a resonance of a high vibration, and her knee responded.

At the end, I held the intention for Cheryl to experience Grace in all areas of her life, something she herself had talked to me about as one of her favorite techniques for healing. Cheryl was thrilled with the healing. She later reported that her knee definitely felt better. It was an encouraging start.

With each healing I did after that, I developed more skill at holding the highest resonance and setting a strong, clear intention. If someone had an illness, I would hold an intention to heal the illness. I would also try to heal all underlying causes, as well. If someone had multiple issues, I held an intention to heal each issue.

Early on, I discovered that it is always good to ask a person what *their* intention is. When someone stated their intention, it gave me a lot more insight into what they wanted and what they believed was possible. You might think that a person who has cancer would want to heal the cancer. But a person might say: "I want to understand why I am sick." Is that because they don't believe they can get better? Or is it that knowing the cause of the illness is in their mind, the key to healing it?

One strikingly beautiful young woman I worked with long after I became a healer illustrates how important the intention is. She and her husband had been trying for years to get pregnant. Doctors had never found a medical reason for their infertility.

"Let's hold the intention for a radiant, healthy pregnancy with ease and grace," I suggested. I felt she could get pregnant very easily and I was excited to help make that happen for her.

"No," she replied. "I want to know why I'm not getting pregnant."

"Are you sure?" I asked. "Don't you just want to get pregnant?" She insisted on her intention.

As soon as I laid hands on her, I could see why. "Does your husband desire you?" I asked gently.

She burst into tears. "Even on our wedding night it wasn't the way I imagined it would be," she recalled. "I thought it would be our special time together. He wanted to party all night with our friends."

Thanks to her clear intention, she had gotten her answer. She needed to accept the marriage as it was, or, I sensed, there might be a different man for her who could be more of a husband on all levels.

A S I STUDIED the nature of intention, I began to see how it is key in creating our lives. I remembered an intention I set when I was between my freshmen and sophomore year in college. I took a clerical job for a company that published a magazine called *Family Weekly*. Each week I read the magazine with great interest as I sat at my desk in a little area that was clearly a "pink" ghetto of female typists and clerical workers.

As I read, I immersed myself in the glittering world of the magazine's pages. I envied the writers, for they were the window on to this world, the keepers of some magical key. One day I announced to the other girls I worked with that I wanted to write cover stories like that for the magazine. "Oh, you'll never do that," one of the older women in our group assured me. "You have to be a well-known writer."

It gave me a chill when I remembered this teenage wish. I had fulfilled that intention without even realizing it. *Family Weekly* was the magazine Gannet had bought and renamed *USA Weekend*.

How many other intentions had I set and fulfilled without even realizing it? How many intentions do most of us set and fulfill without even realizing it? And how many times do we set conflicting intentions?

THE MORE HEALINGS I did, the more I came to see that resonance is just as important as intention. Over time it became clear to me that for the most effective healings, one needs to be able to hold a very high state, such as divine love or pure being.

Yet I also had to be able to attune to many lower frequencies. For instance, in a healing I might connect to someone's fear or anxiety in order to transmute it into peace or faith or trust. I had to become strong enough to set the resonance.

As I did healings, I also continued to clear my own energy field through meditation and healings. Energies like fear and love and anger became tangible to me the way noise or smell or colors would be to most people. I realized that I had always felt energy frequencies. I just hadn't known what I was doing or paid much attention. In fact, I realized we are all highly developed resonating devices. Most of us just aren't conscious of what we're picking up from others or what we are transmitting.

In the beginning, of course, I thought the key to healing might be where the healer put his or her hands. But resonance and intention were far more important. I saw that good healers work with the very forces that shape our lives.

CHAPTER 25

Egyptian Mysteries

E VERYONE TOLD ME I had to interview Henry, that he was such a gifted healer and clairvoyant. I resisted at first because he didn't fit into any of the schools of healing on which I was focusing. But I grew intrigued by the assertions. Among the many healings described to me, Henry had helped a woman who had broken her wrist in 17 places. He insisted that she have her doctors take all the pins out so the bones could completely heal. Eventually, hearing this and other stories, I made an appointment to talk to him.

Most of the healers I had encountered so far were former accountants, actuaries, business executives and nurses. There were even a few doctors. Henry was more off the beaten path, both of this world, and some other world. As we chatted in his office on that first afternoon, I noticed that he wore a large Ankh, the Egyptian symbol for life, on a cord around his neck. It shined and had a magnetic quality. I found it hard to pull my eyes away from it. Later, when we got to know each other, he told me that he was a scholar of ancient Egyptian energy methods. He had magnetized the Ankh with his energy.

Slowly at that first meeting, I became aware that Henry was studying me intently. The more he focused on me, the more I felt as if he was seeing me naked, not so much my physical body, but my soul energies. "What are you looking at?" I finally asked.

"Your energy field," he said. "It's in a lot of motion."

"Oh, I've been recapitulating," I explained.

He gestured for me to tell him more. I explained the process. He nodded approvingly.

After the interview came to a natural conclusion, Henry walked me to the door. He then turned and faced me.

"You don't have any idea of who you are. Do you?" he demanded, in a tone that shook me up.

"What do you mean?" I said. *Who was I? Why would he ask such a thing?*

He merely shook his head at this sorry state of affairs. "We'll talk again," he promised as he escorted me to the door.

A S WE DISCUSSED healing in a series of conversations, Henry and I became friends. The first time we planned to have dinner, however, I woke up in the morning and was too weak to get out of bed. My head throbbed. I could barely think. I felt very sick, yet couldn't pinpoint exactly what was wrong.

When I called to postpone, Henry asked, "What did you do to your energy field?"

"What do you mean?"

"It's like you flattened your chakras," he said.

I didn't know how he could see this over the phone but I explained how I had been doing the Recapitulation with unusual intensity.

"You have to be more careful," he said. "The structure of your energy field has collapsed. No wonder you feel sick."

He promised to work on me from a distance. He assured me that with his expert ministrations, I would be fine by dinnertime. I slept all day. To my surprise, I was well enough by that evening to go out.

Over dinner in an Italian restaurant, Henry told me it took several hours to reconstruct my energy system. I knew that he meant well. But how could he have helped me from a distance? From my perspective, I had just slept and gotten better.

Henry kept a close eye on my energy field. He also treated me as an equal, a fellow healer, an initiate into the mysteries. I wasn't quite sure why. He allowed me to glimpse his power in various ways. In one of his classes, he clapped his hands and the force he created shifted everyone into an altered state.

During a taxi ride Henry described an exorcism he had just done. Keenly aware that the driver was straining to hear every fantastical word, I wished I could sink beneath the floorboards of the cab. Wasn't an exorcism something that only happened in horror movies? I wanted to interrupt, to put a stop to Henry's exposition or at least distance myself from it. Henry kept talking as if he was discussing the most normal thing in the world, and as if I, too, spent my days doing that kind of thing.

ONE SUNDAY MORNING I invited Gerda and Henry to meet over brunch. Things started off politely enough. But suddenly Gerda glared at Henry. "Don't you dare repeat your karma with her," she said, wagging a finger at him. Henry seemed to know exactly what she was talking about. He vibrated with a barely controlled anger.

I was appalled by Gerda's outburst. But as she spoke, a dream I had several years earlier popped into my mind. In it I watched two lovers saying good-bye. They were walking on a beach in Normandy in an earlier time, perhaps a few centuries ago. As they parted, a voice-over announced: "And they never saw each other again." After that, I heard another, more urgent voice: "Pay attention. This is important."

Now, sitting in this café, I had an overwhelming feeling that somehow, Henry and I were the two people in the dream.

The rest of breakfast was polite but strained. Afterwards Henry invited me to join him in a nearby bookstore. We walked through the aisles, picking up books and chatting, but not focusing deeply on anything. Finally, he turned to me. "I'm sorry," he said, putting his hand on my shoulder. "I would have told you eventually."

"Told me what?"

"That we had past lives together."

"I don't know what you mean, I don't really believe in that kind of thing," I said, and it was true.

"It can be shocking and should always be dealt with gently," he continued. "Your friend Gerda shouldn't have done that. I would have told you in the right time."

I nodded. I really didn't have anything to say.

"We'll talk about it more," he promised.

When Henry and I got together after that conversation he asserted that he had been a high priest in the time of the ancient Pharaohs. He insisted that we had known each other then and that I had been his mistress. Of course, I couldn't accept such fantastical claims. Nevertheless, I began to have flashes, similar to dream sequences, of Henry and myself in other times and places. It was as if some other dimension had opened up simultaneous to the present moment. It was unnerving and confusing. And I didn't know what to do about it. Or how to stop it.

At first it seemed almost romantic. But as more images came into play, I realized in each dream segment, Henry and I had been lovers and he had left me, often after I became pregnant. But the most unnerving thing about it all was that if I mentioned some episode to Henry he seemed to know exactly what I was talking about.

Was he just playing along? Or was he responsible in some way for this influx into my psyche? Or could there be something to all of these dimensions of reality?

E VEN IN THE here and now, strange things happened around Henry. One evening, I woke up with a start from a dream in which I watched him prostrate his full body before the most radiant light. The next morning I phoned him and described what I had seen.

"Oh," he said. "That wasn't a dream. I was working on your energy field. When I left, you followed me. I went to see Babaji, the holy man in India. You saw me bowing down to him."

"Really?" I said, incredulous. Babaji was someone that Paramahansa Yogananda had described in his autobiography. He was said to have lived for a thousand years or more in the very same body, tucked away high in the Himalayas. I was intrigued that Henry seemed to think that Babaji was real. But traveling to see him? I had never heard of anything like it. "How could I follow you?" I asked.

"It's easy," he said. "With your subtle body."

"Well, how do I do that?"

"Come on," Henry said. "You already know. You don't need me to tell you. "

I didn't know what Henry was talking about. But he glossed right over that.

"Listen," he continued. "I am going to go to ancient Egypt tonight. Do you want to come?"

"Yes, " I said. What did I have to lose? I wondered what could possibly happen.

That night I had a bizarre dream. I was traveling with a companion who brought me into a big round cathedral space. It was in use, yet it also had the feeling of being like a museum, housing something from the past. Everyone was crowded around the center where there was an altar. As we drew close, I realized everyone around me was chanting. "I didn't know anyone still spoke this language," I said excitedly to my companion. Then I woke up.

Was that Egypt? I didn't know.

I OFFERED TO DO a healing for Henry. "You can work on me anytime," he told me. "You have beautiful, soft energy." But when I realized that a healing or two wasn't going to end the seeming hallucinations, I began to recapitulate the dream images that involved Henry.

I went to see my first healer, Dianne, to gain more clarity. When she took me into her healing room, I was stunned. I saw that she had new sheets on her table and they had an Egyptian motif.

I would never get to the root of everything Henry claimed. But one thing did become clear. Apparently I knew more than I thought I did about traveling with my subtle body, as I was about to discover in the most unexpected way.

CHAPTER 26

Ceremony of Light

I N THE ARATI ceremony performed in temples across India, lights are waved to the Teacher or deity. At the New York meditation center I attended, the girls performing the ceremony always looked like the Goddess Lakshmi, the Goddess of Abundance. They wore beautiful saris, did their make-up perfectly, and had their hair pulled back. They seemed radiant, full of *shakti* or divine energy, and completely transformed from their ordinary personality. I wished I could be one of these women.

One day, the woman in charge of the Arati invited me to be one of the girls who performed this ceremony, almost as if she had read my mind. "You have a good *bhav*," she said.

"*Bhav?*" I asked.

"Focus on the Teacher. A good energy."

Her assessment surprised me. I didn't feel especially focused on the Teacher. Still, I was glad she felt that way. She was a former stylist for *Vogue*. She had a very precise, focused energy. It was clear that she was the reason the girls always looked so impeccable.

I said I would love to do it. I had my own sari, made of sheer, white silk with gold threading. I had loved it from the moment my mother gave it to me, but I had never had a reason to wear it. She had brought it back as a gift from India, where she and my father had gone on vacation.

Betty, a woman who regularly performed the Arati, showed me what to do. We did special mantras to purify ourselves before we started. After that we prepared the offering tray, adding a little dish of sacred substances, a perfect red rose, and a candle made with ghee. Then we carefully dressed in our saris. In a sense, we were part of the offering.

Betty was gracious and welcoming. In a little synchronicity that I found comforting, like me she had also gone to Barnard College. That first morning Betty decided we would both perform the ceremony. She would go to the front of the hall. I would stay in the back, waving the sacred flame to a picture of the Teacher's Teacher. It seemed like the less glorious position. Despite my doubts about worshiping the Teacher, this concerned me. I always wanted to be well-positioned. Still I had a very beautiful experience. Tears of devotion welled up in my eyes. It was much more intense than I expected.

The very next morning, I had the dream:

> *I was standing before the Teacher, dressed in my white and gold sari, with my hair pulled back, wearing the most perfect makeup and a red bindi, or dot, on the spot where my third eye would be. We were alone, just myself and the Teacher. I was waving the tray with the sacred flame in devotion to her, just as I had done at the meditation center.*

When I came out of the dream, I looked at the clock. I had performed the Arati at exactly the time it was done in the ashram.

I didn't know how I had ended up before the Teacher. But it was no ordinary dream. I knew without a doubt that I had really been in the presence of the Teacher.

CHAPTER 27

Awakening My Light Body

“**I**F YOU AWAKEN your light body, you'll be able to *see*,” my friend Thomas Ayers told me one day.

“Really?” I asked.

“It's what enabled me to get through healing school,” Thomas assured me. “The chakras, the energy vortexes, are like a broom closet compared to the vast expanse of your light body.”

Thomas had awakened his light body through a course developed by an organization called Luminessence. He recommended that I do the same, under his tutelage.

The Light Body, he explained, was a way to access the seven vibrational energy centers, which correlate to the chakras. Yet as important as the vibrational energy centers are, in a way they were just preparation for awakening the three centers of the Light Body, an energy field more subtle than the aura. The implications for healing work were enormous, he claimed.

While you could do all kinds of things in the aura that would have a global effect on a person's body and on their life, Thomas told me that I would have an exponentially greater effect when working in the Light Body. It was more fundamental, more causal, than even the aura. Working at this level could create very profound results.

The greatest result of all, however, would be the transformation of my own consciousness, according to Thomas. My ability to perceive would be greatly expanded. Instead of just perceiving at the physical level, I'd be able to perceive energies at these fundamental levels.

I trusted Thomas, a gentle soul. Thomas was a thoughtful, complex person who had extended a deep nurturing friendship to me. Spiritually he had what I thought of as a difficult awakening. He had spent a year sobbing his heart out when he first began studying Kriya Yoga with the Self Realization Fellowship because the energies stirred up so much. He still meditated every day. He had served in the Army's Special Forces during Vietnam and continued to work part-time at the Pentagon, where he had a high security clearance. He was also studying to be a psychotherapist. He was very bright and intellectually dexterous yet had delved into spiritual philosophy and practice deeply.

Thomas was someone I could count on. Once, when I felt for sure that my life was dissolving, I called him in the wee hours of the night. He was the only person who I knew would be awake. He was also one of the only people with whom I felt I could talk. I told him that perhaps I needed immediate psychiatric help. I felt like I couldn't handle my situation any longer. I obviously had no power to change it, no matter how desperately I tried. It was one thing to watch *The Twilight Zone* on TV. It was another thing to be living it. I asked him if he thought I should check myself in somewhere.

"You're just having a spiritual crisis," he assured me. "It's okay. It will pass." And indeed, it did.

FOR MY INITIATION into Light Body, we met at the Egyptian Obelisk behind the Metropolitan Museum of Art in Central Park. It was a beautiful late spring day. Everything was radiantly green and in bloom. The park smelled of wet, rich earth and the sun shone bright and clear.

We walked around the obelisk, admiring the ancient hieroglyphics and its majestic height. It survived from an era before Christ to the late 20th century and had journeyed from Egypt to America. It looked out over the Metropolitan Musuem of Art where, in the Temple of Dendur, another paean to ancient Egypt, some of the ritziest parties in New York were hosted, parties that I might have been going to if I had continued writing *The Daily News* society column. But that seemed like a faint memory now. As we basked in the obelisk's mystery, I felt as if I had known Thomas forever, all the way back to the time when the obelisk had been new.

We sat down in its shade. Thomas began to chant a series of strange sounding words that electrified me. Years later, when I taught Light Body for the first time, I realized he had been repeating the vibrational sound of each energy center and the three light body centers. Then he smiled at me and handed me a volume of tapes. "Listen to these tapes, and let's talk as you go along. I'll be transmitting to you."

THE TAPES PUT me to sleep. I had to listen to each of them several times. Then, to actually hear what was on them, I finally listened to them as I took my walks along the East River.

"That's okay," Thomas laughed when I told him. "It's not really sleep. It's a shift in your consciousness. You're still getting what's on the tapes." It was hard to grasp how this could be. I had always assumed my intellect was the star of the show.

It took me almost a year to open my light body. As I made my way through the tapes and had different experiences, I always had Thomas to turn to discuss and analyze and integrate my experiences. At first, the energy exercises to open the light body seemed rather tedious. Slowly I realized the process was having a dramatic effect. The first time I noticed this, I was at a chant. When I ran my first three centers, a jolt of energy ran all the way up my spine as if I had plugged myself into an electric outlet.

After that, I was always experimenting to see what effect running these energies would have. I found that even in the supermarket, if I ran my energy centers as I waited on the checkout line, everyone around me would grow more peaceful. Another time, I went into a store to return an alarm clock and encountered a difficult sales clerk. It occurred to me to run the energy from my heart center. It was like turning on a light switch. The sales clerk became pleasant and helpful. I was able to notice the effects of my energy on the world around me long before I began to really grasp their effect on me directly.

Still, learning these energies was like learning a new alphabet, or the notes of a musical scale. Once I learned these notes, the possibilities were infinite. I could, over time, read almost anything as energy. I could also work with the energy of people, places, situations, objects and events. Everything was made of this energy.

As I worked with the energies, my conscious awareness expanded. I was able to maintain a higher flow state and it radiated through my life. It also expanded my perceptions and understanding. Soon I developed the ability to transmit harmony to others, as well.

Eventually, I could use each of my centers as a sensing mechanism, much the way we use our hands to touch the physical world and our eyes to scan the visible light spectrum. I could literally feel the flow or contraction in other people's energy centers simply by running my own energy centers and creating a resonance.

Ultimately I was able to use the energy from my heart center to calm and soothe other people. In healings, I would hold an expanded state and invite the person I was working with to rest their heart in my heart. Once we had connected heart to heart, soul to soul, I could go in and do very deep work.

AT A WRITER'S conference hosted at a small liberal arts college in New England, I had an experience that showed me just how much I was expanding. It was a bucolic setting. The crisp, pure country air smelled of pine, and the rolling lawns were a deep green color.

My dorm room had a rubber mattress. Every time I turned in bed, the sheets slid around. Even worse, when I tried to sleep that first night, I could hear every word of a conversation taking place four flights below my window, where two men were talking.

Listening to them drone on, I grew increasingly angry. Finally to soothe myself, I began to meditate and run my energy centers. I dropped into a deeper and deeper state. At some point I expanded out so much that this man who talked incessantly was now inside my energy field. I sensed his terrible loneliness. I felt only love and compassion and union.

With my heart's energy I touched his heart and let him know that he was loved. A moment later he was saying good night to his friend. It was an ecstatic experience of oneness. And it had happened by accident.

CHAPTER 28

Pure Presence

W ITH LONG GRAYING hair and luminous blue eyes, Jason Shulman looked like an old-testament prophet. He had delved into the Kabbalah and, after first studying with Barbara Brennan, founded his own school, A Society of Souls, S.O.S for short, a life-saver for souls.

I joined one of Jason's classes at the Cathedral of St. John the Divine, just blocks from where I had gone to college on the Upper West Side. Jason taught us how to work with the Sh'ma, the most holy prayer in the Jewish canon, to bring in the light of pure presence, in what he so poetically called *The Healing of Immanence*.

He demonstrated the healing with a volunteer, a Lutheran minister who literally began vibrating under Jason's hands as we all watched. The minister said afterwards that he had felt Spirit palpably for the first time in his life. He was shaken and inspired by the experience.

Then Jason gave us instructions, explaining that as we prayed the Sh'ma, we created a space for direct illumination. As we did this, we should also witness the divinity of the person on whom we were laying hands.

I paired up with a man named Isaac, who said he wanted to work on his marriage. When I laid hands on him and silently chanted the Sh'ma, I had a vision of him with the Wailing Wall behind him. As I went deeper, I held the light of divinity for Isaac and his marriage. I saw that he felt the only way his wife would love him is if could earn a good living. I showed him during the healing that he could be loved for himself.

As part of the workshop, Jason asked us to contemplate the things with which we couldn't make peace and witness their divinity. It had never occurred to me to see my problems as divine, as a gift. It turned everything around for me.

After that, no problem was too big or too painful—or too small—to turn over to God. When something happened that upset me, I prayed the Sh'ma or repeated my mantra over and over again. These ancient, ritualized prayers provided a ready-made intent, an intent of the highest order, the intention to connect to the Absolute. They also carried a very high resonance, a resonance of love and union. Almost without fail, something would soften. A new way of perceiving would open up.

Sometimes the problem would literally evaporate, solved in some mysterious way. Other times, the higher purpose of the issue would become clear. Everything I offered in prayer became fuel for the fire that was burning away deep obstacles, limiting beliefs and anxiety.

I realized prayers and mantras are like a superhighway to the Divine. They take us to a very high place when done with focus and devotion. With prayer, I was tapping into the sound body of God. Through prayer we can connect to divine love, the pure Presence. This divine love has nothing to do with desire or attachment. It just radiates, like the sun radiates light. It is the source of all healing.

GIFTS OF THE SPIRIT

CHAPTER 29

The Lake

I FOUND THAT I loved being on retreat with the Teacher. There was, in my mind, only one little problem with "vacationing" at the ashram. There was no lake for me to swim in. I loved to swim, so this "flaw" was very much on my mind as I went for a visit in late June in 1996.

I was looking forward to this visit as a respite from my worries. I was waiting anxiously for my second agent to do his magic. So far things weren't looking too promising and my bank reserves were dwindling. All my career hopes were pinned to my book. I had no idea what would happen to me if I didn't sell it.

The trip to the ashram started off on a bumpy note. I was so intent on getting there that I drove over the speed limit in my borrowed car. A patrolman pulled me over to ticket me and I ended up being later than I had planned.

Then, as if someone was trying to teach me a lesson, when I got to the registration desk, the girl who checked me in asked me to step aside for a few minutes. I ended up being detained for well over an hour. I knew what the problem was. On my very first visit to the ashram, I had listed my occupation on a form as "journalist." Nobody had ever referred to my stated profession on any subsequent visit. But this girl suddenly decided I needed "special" handling. By the time a senior supervisor came to speak with me,

I was fuming. I vowed to myself never to visit the ashram again.

Still I was already at the ashram. And I decided to stay this one last time. I offered to serve in the chopping room. I had grown to love offering *seva*, selfless service. When I offered to help there was so much love and so much *shakti*, spiritual energy, that I considered it a form of grace to do even a menial job. Tasks I didn't enjoy in my daily life somehow became fun to do in the ashram. We were asked to perform mantras before we started any task so that everything we did would be sanctified. The place radiated with this pure, divine energy.

In the chopping room, the supervisor would introduce the vegetable we would be chopping and demonstrate how the cooks wanted it to be prepared. Then we would chop buckets of the vegetable, each of us cutting the zucchini or broccoli in the exact same way. As we worked we might talk about transformation or experiences we had had with the Teacher. At other times we simply chanted together or chopped in silence. Chopping was often a soothing, even uplifting experience.

When it came time for a break, the man who had been chopping next to me invited me to join him for morning tea. "I want to talk to you," he said. I realized then that he was one of the swamis, someone who had taken vows of renunciation and celibacy.

As we walked over to the little café in the ashram, he assured me that I would indeed publish my book, which I had mentioned to him as we were chopping together. "You just need to clear some things out," he advised. I had no idea what things he was referring to, but that was the end of the conversation.

Soon, others joined our table, and the monk introduced me to a friend of his, Charles, who had been going to the ashram for years. As Charles and I chatted, I mentioned my longing to swim.

"Oh, there are a lot of lakes nearby," Charles told me. "Why don't we meet at lunchtime? We'll drive around and I'll show them to you."

CHARLES GAVE ME the grand tour, saving the best lake for last. Sunset Lake was so close to the ashram that I could walk to it from my room. A simple little path took us directly from the road to the beach.

It was a beautiful lake that was ringed by trees and hidden from the road, giving it a private, secluded feeling. There was just one house on the entire lake. We sat down by the shore on the beach, watching the still blue glaze of the water. In the distance, marsh grasses and lily pads grew along the shore and a few ducks swam here and there.

Charles broke the silence. "It's all real," he said, referring to the Teacher, still gazing out at the water. His Teacher in the early days was the Teacher of the current Teacher.

"What do you mean? How do you know?" I asked. I knew I needed to listen carefully.

"I've seen it," he said.

"Seen what?"

"The power. It's real."

"What did you see?"

He paused, picking at the grass. "The Teacher asked me to become a swami."

"But you didn't do it?"

"No. I wanted to get married," he said. He had already told me that he had been married and was divorced. I wondered if he regretted the choice, considering how it had turned out. But I didn't interrupt to find out. I never got to ask him because what he spoke about next made everything else irrelevant.

"The Teacher gave me initiation. I can't even begin to describe what happened," he continued. "It was so dazzling, so incomprehensible. I had a moment where I knew everything. I still can't make sense of it. The Teacher told me it would take me many years to understand the experience. I am still absorbing it. I am not even close."

We fell silent again and looked out on the water. I had the sense he had been shattered by the experience in some way. I wanted to ask more. But I couldn't form any questions. Still, I knew that his experience was related to the experience I had when the Teacher had sent that tsunami wave through me. My life too had been irrevocably shattered in that moment.

Ever since then I had been obsessed with God and the Divine Light. I used to gobble up novels and movies like so many bonbons, and snack on dozens of magazines at a time. Now I could only read books by the Teacher or books about spiritual light. I would read the same books over and over again to glean whatever I could, and sometimes, just to feel comforted.

I wanted illumination. I wanted to merge into that light. It was as if, in that moment with the Teacher, the membrane that separated me from the Divine had been ripped apart and now I was trying to catch up with that cataclysmic change.

After awhile Charles spoke again, changing the topic.

"Originally, we were forbidden to swim here. But then the Teacher asked the Brahmin priests to do special mantras at the lake and now it is purified. You can swim here."

That afternoon at Sunset Lake with Charles was a gift. The Teacher had heard the inner longing of my heart. I knew I had her blessing to swim. I also knew that Charles was a messenger on other levels, as well.

On subsequent visits I often swam the entire length of the lake during my lunch break, even when I was on my feet eight or ten hours a day serving in the kitchen. I always sent my inner gratitude to the Teacher.

CHAPTER 30
Grace

SUE AND I were eating lunch outside at a picnic table at the
ashram. It was a hot sunny day in July. Tall trees shaded the
area. The gentle lawn spreading out all around us was a deep
crisp green. I had only just met Sue, a young college grad on
staff there. She had called me at home to invite me to lunch
after hearing about the way I had been detained at registration on my
most recent visit.

As nice as Sue had been on the phone, I never expected to return.
But mysteriously, there I was. A friend had called and offered me a ride
and I decided to take her up on it. In a way, it was a relief. I had just
found out that my book had been rejected by nearly every publisher—
for a second time. I was in need of solace and guidance. At least, it was
soothing to be on the ashram grounds and away from my problems in
New York.

Sue, making casual conversation, asked me what I did for a living. I
burst into tears. I was mortified, crying in front of a girl who was a good
decade younger than me. But I couldn't help myself.

When I pulled myself together, I explained about my book, which I
had been working on now for several years. I confessed that on top of that
rejection, I also couldn't get work as a journalist and I didn't know what
to do next.

"You need to have *darshan* with the Teacher," Sue said. She took me over to the hall where the Teacher was offering *darshan* and brought me to the front of the line, which parted for us like the waters of the Red Sea. As Sue explained my situation, the Teacher seemed to lean forward, or maybe I just imagined that. But she did take my hand into her hands and slipped something into it, then closed my hand around it.

The Teacher was so friendly, her eyes danced. Normally, she seemed so distant and aloof. "Go to the Temple and ask *Paramahansa* for help," she told me. *Paramahansa* was the grandfather of the lineage. The honorific meant Great One. He was also sometimes affectionately called "Great or Grand Father" in an Indian dialect.

"But I've already done that."

"Well," the Teacher said, "go do it again." She winked at me. She was in a very good mood.

"DO YOU THINK this will help?" I asked Sue afterwards. "Absolutely," she replied. Still, she cautioned: "It doesn't mean your book will sell. But I am sure you will receive the Teacher's help. Whatever happens will be what's best for you."

When Sue and I parted, I opened my hand to see what the Teacher had given me. My heart sank. I was clutching a little plastic statue of Hanuman, the God of the Wind and the King of Selfless Service. Hanuman was a monkey with wings. Why couldn't she have given me a little statue of the beautiful Lakshmi, the Goddess of Abundance? Lakshmi was a radiant goddess. I wasn't aware then that I was always measuring what I got and thinking I had come up short. Still, I reminded myself that the Hanuman statue was a gift from the Teacher and I held it tightly. I told myself I would understand more about the meaning of it later.

I went directly to the Temple. In meditation, I silently laid out the entire situation to *Paramahansa* all over again, as if I was talking to a person instead of a statue. Then I walked around the temple, and when I came back in front of *Paramahansa*, I bowed in thanks. Just in case.

I went home still feeling desperate. I even called Mother Meera to get her guidance. She was a Divine Mother, and I knew she would give wise advice. "Mother says you must get a job," came the reply through her secretary, in her lilting, Hindu-tinged English.

A FEW WEEKS LATER I realized I had undergone an astonishing transformation. My debilitating panic was gone. I had no idea when or how it left. It had mysteriously evaporated without my noticing. My mental and emotional states were much lighter. Now I knew with utter certainty that I would get another job, even if it was not my dream job. There were millions of jobs out there. Why had I ever despaired?

I no longer felt my life depended on whether or not I published my book. Rather, I felt enormous gratitude for the opportunity to do the research for it. What I had seen and learned was priceless. How many people got to learn from such extraordinarily talented healers in private interviews? It hardly mattered whether I got a contract or not.

As time went on, I saw that my state was permanently altered. I would never have that type of worry and desperation about work again. I would always know that when something didn't come to me, it simply wasn't meant to be.

I knew then that the Teacher had helped me. She and Paramahansa had done something to lift me out of my terrible darkness. I had experienced extraordinary Grace. The Teacher's power to heal and transform was astounding and unfathomable. I felt certain now that she was my Teacher, just the way people know when they've met the person they will marry. I didn't know how I had gotten so lucky to find her. But I knew that there was a deep commitment and it went both ways.

From the books I had read, I knew that according to ancient Indian scriptures known as the *Vedas*, when a truly enlightened Teacher initiates you, she guides you all the way. She helps you to release all your karma—what we might call patterning and delusion. I had seen that this could be true. I wanted more of that kind of help, as much of it as I could receive.

I wrote a flurry of letters to editors, seeking a job. In the midst of this job seeking, my agent called to let me know that he now had two publishers who were going to make final offers for my book. It wasn't exactly a bidding war. Yet, it looked like there was hope for my project.

On the day that my agent handled final negotiations with the two publishers, I couldn't bear waiting by the phone. I got on my bicycle and ended up at the very southern tip of Manhattan in an area of Battery Park where

I had never been. I ran right into a statue of my raptor, in the form of an eagle. It towered over me. Altogether, with the pedestal, it must have been almost 20-feet high. When I returned home my agent called and updated me. Feeling I had been given the nod by my raptor, I followed my agent's recommendation and took the offer from Hampton Roads, which specialized in books on healing, spirituality and metaphysics.

I had always believed that my state was based on outer events. Now I knew that what the yoga books said was true: The outer world was a reflection of my inner state. I marveled at my new state and, also, at just how deluded I had been.

"Everything unfolds in the perfect way," the Teacher had said. I had never believed it. Now I could see, everything did happen for the best! Getting detained at registration, which had made me so furious, led to the meeting with the Teacher, which had completely rearranged me from inside.

When I saw the girl from registration—an ordinary-looking girl—I was overcome with gratitude and love. She had played such a major role in my getting the help I needed. I wanted to reach out and hug her. The only thing that stopped me was that she didn't even recognize me.

CHAPTER 31
The Hollywood Bible

"**C**AN YOU HOLD for Peter Bart?" the secretary's voice said. A moment later, Peter Bart, the editor of *Variety* and an iconic figure in Hollywood, was on the line. "I got your note about coming to work for *Variety*," he said. "Let's have tea."

The following week we had afternoon tea at the luxurious Mark Hotel on New York's Upper East Side. Tea was very civilized, with pots of steaming black tea, and a bountiful spread of dainty little finger sandwiches and pastries. Peter, who had once been a studio exec, couldn't have been more debonair. He put me at ease immediately as we talked about Hollywood, the business of movies and journalism.

Peter was a true Hollywood power broker, a maestro. He generously shared tips about what he had learned on the way to the top, along with entertaining anecdotes, and turned the conversation to actors we both knew. For instance, I had interviewed Ali McGraw just a few years earlier when she came out with a yoga dvd, and he had known her in her acting heyday, when he had helped produce "Love Story," the movie that had launched her. He still kept in touch and filled me in on what she was doing.

Eventually the conversation turned to Manhattan, a city we both loved. It turned out that Peter had once lived in my Gramercy Park neighborhood, just a block from my apartment, in a building I passed almost every day.

It was a magical afternoon. I felt redeemed. Why had I ever worried that my journalism career was over? As we finished up our tea, Peter offered me a job. I was thrilled. But I was sure my pending book contract would nix the offer. Instead Peter became a real-life guardian angel.

"If you're going to write a book, you're going to need money," he observed. "Let me make an arrangement for you. I'll put you on contract. You can work part-time while you work on your book. It takes money to write a book."

For the first time in years, I felt I could relax. The same safety I felt inside the ashram was beginning to permeate the rest of my life.

Peter put me to work as an editor for the special sections, where I had a lot of flexibility in managing my time. He also assigned me occasional stories for the main publication, with an eye for my sensibility and strengths. For instance, he had me do a story on top agents in New York, sending me to meet all the movers and shakers, including one very senior agent who had represented Carson McCullers, one of my all time favorite writers, along with actors Elizabeth Taylor and Richard Burton. It was a delight to work with Peter. He "got" me. There is something mystical and magical about a well-matched editor and writer, like a *pas de deux*, a ballet for two, but expressed through the written word.

When Peter assigned me to attend several big movie premieres, my old and new worlds began to converge. I invited Trudy, a healer, to accompany me to one of these. I had always marveled at Trudy's clairvoyance. She once told me she had seen faeries as a little girl, inviting me to at least consider that they might be real.

At the dinner, I asked her to scan various people. To my surprise, she gave me the same readings I would have given. Trudy talked about people's chakras. I talked about emotional dynamics. But we were seeing the same things.

I could see that the movie publicist was emotionally unbalanced. There was a man who had been paralyzed in a freak accident and it was clear he was going through a spiritual awakening—and not by choice. The young man tagging along with the famous playwright didn't appreciate the playwright's sexual advances, but enjoyed being close to the limelight.

"You don't realize it," Trudy said. "But the way you see is much better than just seeing the aura. I wish I had your kind of vision. When I see the aura, I still have to interpret it. The way you *see*, you just *know*. You have what's called *Direct Knowing*.

LANDING THE JOB at *Variety* brought a compelling resolution to one of my many ongoing experiments into the nature of reality. For at least a year before I arrived at *Variety*, I worked with a tape series called "Creating Money," produced by Luminessence, the same group that had developed the Light Body course. It taught skills for manifesting and clearing limiting beliefs and other energy blocks. The entire time, I wondered: *Could I create my reality? Could I receive what I asked for? Was my intent that strong? Did the universe really respond to one's consciousness?*

At first, I energized what seemed to me to be a relatively large sum of money. After months passed without any result, I dropped my request to an amount almost 50% lower, thinking I had asked for too much.

My first month at *Variety*, the company sent me two checks instead of one. Combined with the first segment of my book advance, that monthly sum added up to the *exact* amount of money that I had originally energized. Sadly, I had to let the *Variety* accountants know they were paying me double. Soon enough, I was down to one check a month. The new amount, combined with my advance, matched the lower amount I had energized. Exactly.

One had better be careful, I concluded. The universe heard everything and was very precise.

Seeing Auras

T *VARIETY* EVERYTHING was going smoothly, as if grace was handling the details. When Peter flew me out to Los Angeles for a week to meet the West Coast staff, I had a great time. I extended my stay to do research for my book.

While in Los Angeles, I made sure to see the Rev. Rosalyn Bruyere, a healer in Sierra Madre, California, and the head of the Healing Light Center Church. She had taught thousands of people the principles of energy healing, including doctors and nurses in several hospitals, and even post doc students at the University of Arizona Medical School. The Nurse Healers Association has adopted many of her techniques. Even Barbara Brennan briefly studied with Rosalyn.

Before meeting with Rosalyn, I attended one of her workshops to see her in action. She was holding the workshop in a hotel near her healing office in Sierra Madre. I was struck by the ordinariness of the venue. But that was in direct contrast to what I would experience.

As I listened intently to her lecture, I slowly realized I had to pay attention to what I was *seeing*. Almost without realizing it, I had been watching a very bright light behind Rosalyn. The light mesmerized me. At first, I thought it was some kind of spotlight. But after awhile, I realized I was seeing her aura. It was very big and bright. That got my attention. By now,

A CALL TO HEAL   *Seeing Auras* | 111 a big aura was more compelling to me than someone with a big bank account. It showed a true attainment.

Bruyere talked about the energy running through our hands. She said it should have the force of the water in a fireman's hose. She showed us how to pull energy up from the core of the earth. The earth energy was a grounding force, according to Bruyere. Many people who try to do healings only pull energy down from the cosmos. But when the energy also comes through the earth, she explained, it can better impact physical issues.

I had already found that being in a state of prayer or meditation elevated the vibration and power of the healings that I did. But combining that with earth energies meant I could have even more of a physical impact.

After showing us the power of the earth energies, Bruyere then taught the "brain balancing" technique for running energy, a method to harmonize the two spheres of the brain. Soon the energy flowed from my hands with a force that felt physical to me. When I laid hands on another person, I could feel a very powerful vibration, along with heat at my fingertips, as the energy was transmitted. The person receiving the energy could feel it, too, and it resulted in an overall sense of well-being and grace.

That very evening I applied my new skill, laying hands on the first person I could find, a friend who had a headache. I placed my hands on each side of her head. She could feel the energy move through her brain between my hands. Her pain cleared immediately.

From that day on, I was able to very consciously and intentionally run a powerful current from my heart, through my hands and into another person to dissolve pain. Eventually, I would be able to sense how the energy ran through the other person's body. There would even be a special kind of burning sensation in my fingertips when I laid hands right on a physical blockage, illness or trauma.

A FEW DAYS LATER I met Rosalyn in her office to discuss healing. Power emanated from every corner of the room, which was populated with Egyptian icons and two glass cases overflowing with esoteric books on Egypt and healing.

"I saw your aura," I told Rosalyn as we sat down at the window seats. She narrowed her vision to look at a spot between my eyebrows, the location of the so-called third eye. "Well, of course," she said. "Of course, you can *see*."

"No," I said. "I can't. Not usually. That was the first time."

"What do you mean?"

"Well, I can't see your aura now," I said, looking at her to make sure.

"Yes, you can."

"No, I can't."

Rosalyn tried to help me to see, but finally turned to other matters. She talked mostly about her healing "failures," and about the research she had participated in. She seemed to be the opposite of a show-off so I was quite surprised when, as the interview came to a close, she patted her healing table. "Come here," Rosalyn said. "I want to show you something."

As I lay down on her table and closed my eyes, Rosalyn placed her hand on my belly. Soon a powerful vibration went through me as if my belly was a lake and her hand was a motorboat throwing off an enormous wake. I opened my eyes; her hand was utterly still.

"That's a sound vibration," she explained. "Now, I'm going to move to a higher vibration. You won't feel as much."

I didn't really feel anything. After what seemed like just a few minutes, she was done. "Be careful," she said as I got off the table. "You're going to feel a little high." I thought this was ridiculous because she'd only worked on me for what seemed like a few minutes, but of course, I didn't say anything. I didn't want to be rude.

When I got into my car, I saw that four hours had passed while Rosalyn and I had talked. I drove the freeways, getting lost in the tangle of interchanges, enjoying every minute of it, for several hours more. That's when I knew that I was high, very high.

A few days later, I noticed that suddenly, and mysteriously, I had crystal clarity about a particular man in my life. I could see his elusiveness and his inability to stay connected. For the first time, I didn't find him interesting and I didn't want to continue the friendship, let alone see it blossom into something more. I'd had inklings before, but I had never been able to get a grip on what was wrong, or have the fortitude to resolve the situation and let it go.

My new awareness had Rosalyn's fingerprints all over it. I realized that when she had popped me up on her table, she hadn't been trying to show me a frequency. She had seen something in my energy field that she didn't find beneficial for me and she had cleared the energy out. Being able to see an aura was helpful indeed. I didn't have to say a word for her to figure it out and resolve it.

When I saw Rosalyn months later, I thanked her for her help. She knew exactly what I was talking about. "Someone was playing with your second chakra," she explained with a twinkle in her eye.

CHAPTER 33

No Time, No Space

ONE MORNING WHILE I was staying with friends in Los Angeles, I woke with the most terrible migraine headache. I crawled out of bed to call Henry, the healer in New York, and left a desperate message. I didn't know what I thought he could do for me. Offer sympathy? Tell me to put my fingers on a pulse point?

I crawled back into bed, wondering if I would ever be free from the nauseating pain. Soon I noticed a force moving through my body. Was I imagining it? No, I wasn't. My contracted muscles began to relax. They had to obey this force, which felt utterly soothing, as if someone had poured liquid bliss into my veins. I drifted off to sleep.

When I woke an hour later, my headache was gone. I found out later that Henry had sent me healing energy. I had heard about long distance healing, but until then I had never believed it was that powerful or real. Even so, at various times, without fully acknowledging it, I had already benefited from distance healing through Gerda and Henry. Now I wanted to know: *How did they do it?* I had to find out.

"Why don't you give me a long distance healing?" Gerda suggested one day when we were chatting on the phone about the long distance healing I had received while in Los Angeles. Gerda took my interest as an invitation to push my limits. It was something she delighted in doing.

To receive a distance healing was easy. I just lay down, relaxed and let that light, that presence, that peace come to me. It was like someone pouring pure love through my veins. The pain dissolved and I knew that everything was all right.

Doing a long distance healing was another story. "I can't do that," I said. In those days I was constantly having one crisis after another. Magically, Gerda was always there to support me. She had done so many healings for me in person, and sometimes on the phone. I would have liked to reciprocate. But I knew my capacity.

"Just try it," she insisted.

"I can't."

"How do you know until you try?"

"Listen, I just know I can't."

"Well, then it won't hurt to try, will it?"

Who could argue with logic like that? We got off the phone and I lay down and closed my eyes. I got into a very deep, sacred space where I was consumed by love. Then I put my energy hands on Gerda's heart and abdomen. I applied all of my psychic force to this process. All of a sudden, quite unexpectedly, I began to see some very intense scenes from a childhood. At first, I tried to go around them, thinking they were blocking the healing. Finally, I gave up and added light, the only thing I could do.

When I finished the session, I called Gerda. "Nothing happened," I told her.

"Nothing?" she asked.

"Well, I did get this very strange image. But it doesn't make any sense. It had nothing to do with anything."

"Oh?" Gerda said, quite interested. "What was it?"

"Well, it's totally ridiculous. It had to do with some childhood issues." I explained what I had seen. I held my breath.

"That's exactly right," she said, pleased. "That's the issue I'm working on right now. That's what happened to me as a child."

Okay. I could do a long distance healing.

AT FIRST, LONG distance healing remained an exciting but terribly unsettling idea. How could I transmit energy across state lines or across the country? What did it say about the nature of reality?

And how could it be so easy? I knew in accepting long distance healing, I was leaving the safety of the "known" world, the world I had grown up in. Yet, it felt as if I had been born to connect this way.

I was comforted by the findings of quantum physics, which determined in the early 20th century that the behavior of particles in one location *instantaneously* affect the events in another location, as if the particles are linked and know what is happening elsewhere.

"All of the 'parts' of the universe are connected in an intimate and immediate way previously claimed only by mystics and other scientifically objectionable people," explains Gary Zukav in *The Dancing Wu Li Masters*.

I did as many long distance healings as I could with friends and healers from all over the country. It was wonderful to know that help was only a phone call away; that the Grace of loving and empowered friends was always available. The energy was opening me so rapidly that I dove into all the things I wanted to transform.

I learned a tremendous amount by offering healing energy to others in this way. It was extraordinary to work with friends who were gifted healers. They gave me great feedback. I could track their energy, and learn different things about healing from each one of them. Each healer's energy was distinct and unique, but a healing from any one of my friends would always shift whatever needed to be shifted. And I was always amazed at how powerful the effects would be when I transmitted to others. How could something that simple and fun be so profound?

In these soul planes, distance simply did not exist. I was able to tune in immediately. I could feel what was going on inside someone else's body as if it was in my body. I could even feel the other person's heart beat inside my own heart. I could usually, but not always, tell if someone's mind was racing or if the energy lulled a person into an altered state or even put someone to sleep.

I found it easy and quite blissful to bring someone else's heart to rest in mine, even at a distance. For me, that heart connection was the doorway to oneness. Then I could work on other things, from back pain to anxiety to preparing someone for surgery.

I learned as I went. I quickly discovered that I could pick up medical and metaphysical issues, even when people didn't mention them to me. Once I did a distance session with a woman who wanted me to focus on balancing her right and left sides. I found that the imbalance began in her heart. The energy wouldn't "let" me do anything except balance her heart.

"Gee, that's so amazing," the woman said afterwards. "I've been feeling this discomfort in my heart, almost like I had a kind of murmur. And I totally forgot to mention it to you." She added, "You know, I had open-heart surgery a decade ago. That feeling in my heart was making me so anxious. Thank you so much. That was just what I needed." The discomfort in her heart disappeared after the healing and never returned.

Another time, I worked with a healer who said he wanted to experience more connection to the spiritual light within. At first I felt like I couldn't connect deeply. I realized that it was this resistance that he needed to heal. I held light and burned off his resistance.

With each healing I did, my "library" of experience expanded. The more feedback I got, the more I began to trust myself and the energy. As I did long distance healings, I became less worried about the science behind it. It was something I came to accept, in the same way that I don't worry about how electricity works when I turn on a light switch. From my experiences, it was clear that some part of us exists in a quantum or soul domain, connected beyond time and space.

Eventually, I was able to pick up very fine "physical" details in my long distance work. After putting light on a bladder infection for a parapalegic man, I ran energy through his spine. As I did, I realized I didn't know where on his spine his injury had occurred. Then, almost right at the bottom of it, I found a break where the energy didn't move through. The man's daughter confirmed that the injury had occurred very near the base of the spine.

Long distance healing taught me a lot about the soul. Once, as I was transmitting light to an editor at *Variety*, one of my former magazine bosses came to me in his etheric form.

A few days later I picked up the newspaper and learned he was involved in a titanic battle for control of a big media asset. Somehow, I had been dispatched to work with him soul to soul.

From these experiences my trust in the Teacher grew stronger. I knew without doubt that she could help people, including me, beyond time and space. Truly there is no separation. We are one.

CHAPTER 34

Turning Up The Flame

CCORDING TO INGRID, receiving the Teacher's grace was simple: Just show up, focus on the Teacher, and serve. She said that she sat at the back of the hall and hardly ever spoke to her Teacher. Yet she had been transformed.

I had been following Ingrid's guidance. Then I went for a Christmas retreat in 1996. I took the bus to the country with two healers, who were surprised to discover I was going to the ashram just to relax.

"But what will you do all day?" asked Susan Weiley.

"I don't know," I said. "Read?"

I saw the look on her face. "I've never been bored," I explained. "I just go and hang out. It always works out fine. Maybe I'll go and wash some dishes."

"Well," said Susan. "I guess that works for you." She did not sound very convinced.

At the ashram, I ran into Jake, a tall, young guy with whom I felt deeply, if inexplicably, linked. Jake was totally devoted to the Teacher. He would work a job for awhile and then quit to follow the Teacher on a meditation and teaching tour. Then he would take another job, and so it would go. He had done trucking and shifts at McDonald's. I found his faith mesmerizing. I didn't think that I could ever live that way.

"Are you taking the meditation retreat?" he asked, sitting down next to me at the dinner table where I was dining with my friends.

"No," I said.

"You should," he said.

"Really?"

"Yes. Really."

Somehow I knew that I was hearing the voice of the Teacher. Perhaps it was the extra resonance in Jake's words. Whatever it was, I felt guided to sign up for the intensive retreat, where the energy was said to be especially concentrated and powerful.

On the morning of the retreat I took my seat in the hall—a tiny, square patch of space on the floor. Almost as soon as the program started, I began to cry. I sobbed the entire day, stopping only during the pauses. I had no idea until then that I had so much sorrow inside of me. And even then I couldn't say why I was so sad.

To hide my crying, I covered my head with the wool shawl I had just bought. I felt terribly ashamed. Yet I could feel compassion and a sense of love from the women sitting near. One neighbor handed me one tissue after another. She seemed to know exactly when I needed the next one.

The next day as soon as the program started, so did my tears. However, by the afternoon my inner sun was shining. I felt a new radiance, as if there had been a harsh storm that had washed away a thick layer of grime and fog.

For a few days after the retreat, I was in a truly great state. Then I fell ill with a migraine headache as I came crashing into my normal state of contraction.

"How are you feeling?" Susan asked, as I sat down to join her and the other healer, Joan Luly, for lunch.

"Not so well," I replied. "Why?"

"Your pancreas is wavering."

"That's interesting. I'm getting a migraine." I seemed to get a migraine whenever I went on retreat with the Teacher. I suspected at times that maybe it was the food in the ashram. Susan almost seemed to read my mind.

"You need to eat some protein," Susan told me. She had packed some protein powder for the trip and sent me to her dorm room so I could make a shake with it, mixing it in a plastic water bottle, without a banana or berries to mask the taste.

"Food is medicine," Susan told me, and I repeated that to myself as I drank it up.

My migraines were like a tornado; they would suddenly descend on me, seemingly out of nowhere, and ravage me. The protein powder wasn't powerful enough to stave off the storm, which really had to do with much deeper issues than protein. The next morning I woke up feeling very ill. Joan, the other healer who I was traveling with, started her day by giving me an energy healing.

After the headache cleared, I came down with a terrible cold. On the bus back to New York, I clutched an enormous wad of tissues. Each time I sniffled, I was embarrassed anew. It seemed like I needed to travel with healers because I needed healing 110 percent of the time. I apologized for being such a mess.

"Oh, don't worry," Susan said. "Just think what a great clearing you're having. This is all great. Imagine how much better you are going to feel soon."

She was right. These illnesses, like most illness, were part of a deep process of purification. Dross was being burned out of me and my whole energy field was recalibrating to a higher vibration.

I took many retreats after that. It seemed as if years of spiritual practice were concentrated into each weekend. I don't know how many buckets of tears I sobbed in the first few years. I didn't know a person could have so much sorrow stored up in them — I certainly didn't know that I did. Generally speaking, I had had a pretty good life.

For the next decade, I ceased wearing mascara because it would always smear, not only during the retreat weekends but with every meditation session I now did.

During the retreats I could only wear the lightest cottons, even in the dead of winter. The fire of the *shakti*, the spiritual energy, was so powerful that I would often feel feverish. Sometimes I had to change my clothes during the lunch break. I was glad that I didn't know very many people in the early days, and that none of them sat right near me. Intensive retreats were, well, intense.

At the end of the retreat, there would be *darshan* with the Teacher. When I came before her, I could never form any spoken words, even when I desperately wanted to ask her for help. I learned to frame a silent intention and hold on to that as I kneeled before her.

Although I wanted many things, I could never articulate anything personal. I ended up asking for the grace to radiate Divine Love. Naively, I thought this would serve as an umbrella request, one that encompassed the earthly love I so longed to experience as a wife and mother.

After the meditation retreat, I always felt more peace and serenity than I had ever experienced in my life. With each of these powerful retreats, bits of mental, emotional and spiritual grime were getting burned up in a spiritual fire that was hotter and brighter than I could imagine. My tears washed away the ashes.

CHAPTER 35

The Tree of Life

A S DANI ANTMAN, a Kabbalistic healer, demonstrated *Tiferet*, the energy pierced my heart. Located at the very center of the mystical Tree of Life, Tiferet can be translated as harmony, balance and beauty. I never expected the energy to be physically tangible. I promptly decided to try a series of Kabbalistic healings.

I felt drawn to explore the Kabbalah partly because of my Jewish upbringing, but also because the *chakra* theory never answered all of my questions. There was a level that went deeper than the *chakras*. I had learned that from opening my light body.

The Tree of Life has ten *sephirot*. The *sephirot* are lights or emanations of God. In Kabbalistic terms, everything is composed—in varying degrees—of these ten lights, including human beings.

Dani had studied with Barbara Brennan and then with Jason Shulman. We had grown up two blocks from each other and I used to walk to Hebrew School twice a week with her younger brother. But we didn't figure out this connection until we had known each other for quite some time.

Dani used the energies of the *sephirot*. In particular, she focused on rebalancing *Hesed* (loving kindness) and *Gevurah* (judgment, stricture, containment, boundaries). These two energies are at opposite extremes.

You could say that loving kindness has no boundaries and that judgment has a rigidity that is too strict, not yielding enough. An imbalance in these energies has deep consequences. For example, when a parent smothers a child, that child may not learn to stand up for themselves. Then again, when a parent is too stern, the child may grow up trying too hard to please others, and thus be without boundaries

Dani was using these energies to reset my boundaries. After a healing, I had the usual dreamy, sleepy feeling; life's little challenges would mysteriously resolve with ease and grace. Yet, at first, I didn't notice any "big bang" effects.

After awhile I realized the healings were having a global effect. For one thing, I started cleaning all of my closets, cabinets and drawers. Over the next year or so, I eventually re-ordered every inch of my apartment.

I threw out reams of files for stories that I knew I wouldn't be writing. I also got rid of mementos from my travels to Italy and elsewhere, and anything connected to previous boyfriends, including a record player given to me by an ex and all of my records that were associated with him.

I even gave away my black-tie party outfits. Although I loved them, I didn't need them anymore. Besides, I no longer wore black. The color just didn't feel comfortable any more.

I was tearing the weeds out of my life at the roots. I was motivated by a brilliant little book, *Clear Your Clutter With Feng Shui,* from which I learned that clutter is always connected to energy congestion on other levels. If you clear your clutter, you change your life. I am sure that I magnetized the book to me as a result of the healings. And I was so desperate to change my life, I would try anything that made sense to me.

As it turned out, I also reordered my personal boundaries in relationships during this same period. I just couldn't see it until I had done it. But going forward, I could spot other people's boundary issues in a snap. It was almost like seeing drapes that aren't hanging right. I would want, with my heart, to help that person straighten their energies out. I could see how much pain their lack of boundaries was causing them. And I could see that they had no idea what the problem was.

Energy was becoming very solid, very vivid, very literal. Dani noted that I had a natural aptitude for tracking energy. When she discussed energies with me and used them in a healing, I mastered them without effort. Then, I would be able to transmit those frequencies in healings that I did.

The shift I was making as I created this new level of order would ripple far into my future. After I finished cleaning out my apartment, I had a dream in which:

> *My apartment was on fire. Although there were flames everywhere, I had time to decide what I was taking with me. My father was there with me, as if I was moving, instead of running from a life-threatening fire.*

I felt sure the dream was prophetic. That was confirmed when I woke up and grabbed a book by an American-born swami from my night table. Asking for guidance, I immediately opened to the very page where she described a dream she had. In it she was driving on a highway towards her destiny when, all of a sudden, she was surrounded by flames. She said that for years after having that dream, whenever she was going through an intense phase of purification, she would have a vision of being surrounded by flames.

They want my apartment, I thought to myself as I read this passage. At first, I panicked. Where would I go? Then I decided: *Well, they can have it. I don't have to do anything. If they want me out, they will have to figure out where they want me to go.*

Fortunately, it would be quite awhile before it was time to move and by then, I would be ready.

CHAPTER 36

A Flood of Memories

"**T**HINK OF ALL the times in your life when you *saw*," Dani suggested to me one day when I mentioned my flashes of inner vision.

"But I've never been able to *see*," I protested. "This is new."

"Is that really true?" she asked. "Just see what comes to you."

After that conversation, much to my surprise, memories began to emerge of *seeing*. It turned out that *seeing* had always been a part of me, a part I had somehow managed to successfully suppress from my consciousness. But still, the ability to *see* had always been there.

For instance, when I was in college, one of my roommates, Amy, invited me to spend the day with her and another girlfriend, Alicia. When we met up with Alicia, she seemed so unhappy. But I quickly suppressed this observation to get along.

By the middle of the day, however, I was so depressed and exhausted I had to excuse myself. I felt suicidal by the time I crawled into my bed for a nap. I realized then that I had absorbed Alicia's depression, the way a sponge soaks up water. With this epiphany, I began to feel lighter and more like myself.

Another instance of *seeing* occurred shortly after I finished college when I lived in downtown Manhattan in Soho. There was a man who lived on the first floor of my walk-up apartment building who always made me uneasy. My apartment mate, Sylvia, had become friendly with him. It disturbed me but I felt there was nothing I could say or do, especially since my feeling about this guy wasn't rational.

One day, as I was coming home, I passed by his place and the door was open. Sylvia was sitting in the parlor, chatting with him. They invited me in. Uneasily, I accepted the invitation, as much out of concern for Sylvia as anything else. As soon as I began to relax, seemingly out of nowhere, a strange glint of energy escaped from this man towards Sylvia. The glint dissolved an instant later. But I knew at that moment that he was capable of murderous rage.

I left that apartment as fast as I could and waited anxiously for Sylvia's return. When she came home, I begged her never to go into that man's apartment again. "I feel he is dangerous," I told her. I didn't have the words to talk about what I had seen. I knew she thought I was hysterical. But finally, she did promise to be careful.

Ten years later, long after we had each moved away, this man was arrested and charged with murdering his girlfriend.

Seeing couldn't always protect the people I loved. I now recalled that shortly after I graduated from college, I went to visit dear friends, a married couple. The wife was very pregnant with their second child and they were both so happy and excited. As we sat down to a beautiful dinner, I heard a voice in my head that said, "She's going to lose him so early."

"Oh my God," I thought, *"My friend's husband is going to die before his time."* Immediately, I told myself to stop being so crazy.

As it turns out, I slightly misinterpreted the information. Five years later, this couple's son died in an accident. He had been in his mother's womb when I had been given the message about his fate. Why was I told such a thing? I didn't know. I had a sense that the child's death had been pre-ordained. Nothing could have altered it. We may have vision to see, but not the power to change destiny.

It made me think of the ancient Greek tragedy of Oedipus, where the royal parents are told by a wise man that Oedipus will kill his father and sleep with his mother. Even though the king and queen send him to a remote village to be raised without any knowledge of his origins, he grows up to live out his fate. Some things are beyond our control.

L OOKING BACK, I had other flashes of insight that I could never explain, and which I had successfully repressed. Once, I even tried to get help with my abilities. It was during my early days as an investigative reporter. I was hurrying into the NYC subway station at 14th street to catch a train early one morning, on my way to see my therapist.

This was a trip I did every week. Yet this particular morning I had a blood-curdling thought: *What if a stranger came up to me on the platform and threw acid in my face? It could blind me.* I shuddered with fear. The platform was almost completely empty. I felt very vulnerable and unprotected. I tried to shake the fear off, but I couldn't. I dashed into the train as soon as it arrived.

My heart raced when, a day or two later, I read a brief article in one of the local papers about a tragic crime that had just taken place. A strange man had approached a young woman on a subway platform and thrown acid in her face, blinding her.

I dutifully told my therapist about the synchronicity, sure that I had *seen* the event. "Why do you think your vision and that crime are related?" she asked, as if I was completely deluded. "You must stop with this magical thinking." Looking back, I found that response unfathomable.

I now recalled that even as a journalist, I had often read the energy of people and situations. One memory was particularly vivid. Working on one of my first big features as a reporter, I interviewed a top executive at a publishing company. I was escorted into his plush office and took my seat as he wrapped up a phone call from behind his big, sprawling desk.

While I waited, I looked around the room at photos of him and his wife, and then watched him talking on the phone, all scrunched up. *"Oh, he's a masochist,"* I thought to myself.

At that moment, he got of the phone and turned to me. "You have to be a masochist to be in this business," he said, as if he had heard me thinking. I nearly jumped out of my skin.

As it turned out, I had even *seen* as a child. I couldn't have been more than eight when my father took me along to a business meeting for a startup company in which he was thinking of investing.

As soon as I met the CEO, I knew he would lie and hurt people. I didn't have words to express this. Instead, I reprimanded myself for my bad thoughts about another person. When the business went sour, the CEO skipped out on the banks.

After these memories came up, Dani suggested that I keep notes of my psychic impressions as they were happening. It turned out I was receiving psychic impressions all the time.

To realize I had been seeing clairvoyantly my whole life was quite shocking. I had never thought of myself as having such a gift. Indeed, as a young child, I had the impression that there was something wrong with me. Now I realized I had this feeling because I didn't understand my abilities and often people would deny whatever I was feeling from them. As a result, I grew up feeling my perceptions were off and that the world was confusing.

Dani helped me to straighten out quite a lot.

My psychic sensitivity really isn't even that unusual. Everyone has these gifts to one degree or another. They are perfectly normal and natural. Now I watch people *see*, *know* and *hear* all of the time. Like me for so many years, they just have no conscious awareness of what they are doing.

I wish we all had training from childhood. We should naturally follow our inner knowing. It's when we don't listen to the inner self that we invite illness, accidents and difficulties into our lives

CHAPTER 37

Answered Prayers

"PLEASE. PLEASE. PLEASE. Help me," I prayed. The pain from my migraine was terrible. It was after midnight. All around me in the big dorm everyone was asleep.

I had tried to meditate. Then I turned on my side, my stomach and my back to alleviate the pain and nausea. I even got up on my knees and bent over in a yoga posture known as child's pose. Finally, I called on the Teacher. I didn't expect help. I just didn't know what else to do. I was desperate.

Quite suddenly, the Teacher stood before me. I sat up. Gently, lovingly, she sat down beside me and took my face in her hands. With ever so much compassion and love, she stroked my cheek, soothing me, calming me, letting me know that everything was all right. If I ran into her in the hall, I assumed she wouldn't even know my name. Yet here she was, healing me, comforting me with so much love. I was astonished and grateful.

In what seemed like just a moment, I grew calm. She let my head and face go. I thought she would leave. Instead she came and laid down next to me, her entire body cradling my body, spooning me and holding me. I was completely embraced in the gentlest, most sweet love. Until that moment, I didn't know that she cared so much about me. We were so close it was as if we were sisters. She stayed with me awhile, until I felt better. Then she left.

The whole thing was so miraculous and unexpected that I got out of bed to see where she had gone. I didn't see anyone or anything. I realized then that we had been together, just not on the physical plane in my bed. The whole thing had happened on the soul planes and it had been as real as day-to-day life.

Comforted, I fell asleep.

THE NEXT MORNING, the Teacher gave a talk in the main hall. I sat towards the back on the floor, squeezed in between dozens of women and children. It was a holiday program marking the end of the summer and there were hundreds, maybe thousands, of people gathered.

During the program, the Teacher announced that she would no longer offer formal one-on-one sessions with each of us after this or any other program. A distressed murmur went through the crowd. After all, to receive an audience with the Teacher was considered the culmination of many lifetimes of spiritual practice. It was the highlight of any visit to the ashram. It was a sacred moment between Teacher and student. Anything was possible.

The Teacher explained that she had heard someone complaining about waiting on line. Obviously, people didn't appreciate what they were being given. But she assured everyone, she would still meet with us, for instance, in dreams. She said sometimes it was easier to come in our dreams. We weren't so intimidated by her. She said she might even come to see one of us at night and gently stroke our cheek.

Was she talking to me? In an instant, I knew that she was. I knew then that I'd still be having meetings with the Teacher.

It was strange that on some level we were so very connected. I still doubted that she'd recognize me if we passed each other in the hallway.

CHAPTER 38

The Teacher Inside

AS TIME WENT on, I noticed that the Teacher was always guiding me. She spoke to me not only directly, but also through other people, and even events. At first, I recognized this only in the ashram. For instance, one evening I sat in the lounge near the silent dorm wearing my favorite dungaree shirt. It was old and worn and ripped. But I loved it.

A girl tugged on my shirt. When she had my attention, she silently pointed to the torn shoulder of my shirt. Without saying a word, she opened up her chanting book and showed me a line from the morning chant that promised: "*to destroy all sins and end all privations.*" Then she pointed to my ripped shirt again, her gesture indicating that it was a sign of privation, something I might want to shed.

A life without sin or privation. I wanted that with all my heart. I retired that shirt to the back of my closet and finally ripped it up and used it for rags. Going forward, that verse became a promise of the Grace I might receive and I kept it close to my heart.

Another time when I was in the dining hall eating lunch, I noticed that the air was filled with tiny sparkles, a pulsation of light. I only saw the sparkles for a minute and afterwards I wondered if I had imagined them. But deep down I knew they were real. They were sparkles of divine love.

T HE TEACHER OFTEN had specific lessons for me. They could be corrections in my thinking, understanding or behavior. They could also be expansions in my perspective. In these cases, she would seem to dwell within me, as my own wise, higher self. At one point, for instance, the Teacher illuminated my tendency to judge others. I had never even noticed this tendency in myself as it was so natural and normal to me.

At the time, I was serving as a welcome host at the Manhattan meditation center. The woman who coordinated the hostesses moved on to another post. I was invited to take over the hostess team. Even though it was an honor, I declined.

Soon, we had a new team leader, Angie, who rubbed me the wrong way. I had a tendency to be late for our meetings. But now it was almost impossible for me to get to them on time.

After deep contemplation, I realized that she was judging me. The judgment was like a force field, reinforcing my tendency to be late. I was angry to be a victim of her judgments. Yet even with this insight, our relationship continued to deteriorate. Finally, I moved to the flower department where I arranged flowers for the meditation programs.

I continued to meditate on the situation with Angie because I sensed that there was still some insight that was eluding me. Finally, I saw that I had been judging her at least as intensely as she had judged me — for the way she spoke and the clothes she wore. The epiphany sent a chill through me. I had been so angry with Angie, but I was no better than she. I suddenly felt enormous gratitude and love for her. She had been a divine mirror, showing me my own self.

I never discussed my insights with Angie, but she must have sensed the change in my heart. Whenever we ran into each other, we fell into a loving embrace. It was the only way we could express our intense gratitude for each other.

After that experience, I thought I had learned my lesson about judging others, but there was more. One evening, I took the bus home from the meditation center in New York. A woman got on a stop or two after me and sat down across from me. Her clothes were so tight that her flesh bulged. She was overweight. Some of her teeth were missing. *How could she go out looking like this?* I wondered, horrified.

As I continued to size up this woman's unsightly flaws, I heard another voice: *You don't know why she looks this way. Maybe she had an emergency and she had to run out of the house as fast as she could. Maybe she had an illness. Maybe she can't afford new clothes.* Who was I to judge?

As my heart opened, the woman looked directly at me, as if she could sense my newfound compassion. She pointed to an advertisement above my head. It highlighted the plight of battered women. "My husband did this to me," she said to me as if we were alone together on the bus. "He knocked out my teeth. But I got away from him."

That critical, judging voice inside me received a fatal blow in that moment. It never had free reign over me again.

As I surrendered to the process that was unfolding, each new insight into myself, as painful as it might be, created greater and greater freedom from the contractions in my heart and soul and body. To me this was the ultimate form of Grace.

As I surrendered, I grew closer to the Teacher. She seemed more present, more attentive and also more strict. I could not "get away" with anything.

I walked an increasingly narrow path. But the reward, the feeling of being linked heart to heart, soul to soul, was beyond imagining. Once, before a meditation retreat, I heard myself singing in a lucid dream. I was chanting in Sanskrit from a song we would chant in the retreat, asking for an awakening in my heart: *"Let the True Flame burn in my heart."*

Other times, I would pick up one of the Teacher's books before retreat and read a passage or a story from it. A few hours later during the course, the Teacher would tell that exact story. It seemed on some level I couldn't fathom, I was remarkably attuned.

CHAPTER 39

Exchanging Gifts

"I'D LIKE YOU to open my clairaudience," Mariella said, referring to the ability to hear another person's thoughts. We were at a workshop for an energy healing modality called *Flow Alignment & Connection*. Awakening my light body was a requirement for this course. Indeed, the course built on these energies and I experienced just how expansive they could be.

Mariella, a graduate of the Barbara Brennan School of Healing, had just worked on my inner vision. Now, as she lay on the table, I put my hands on her feet and charged her field. Then I worked in her heart. When I felt she was in a deep space, I began running energy into her ears, opening her ability to *hear*.

For the first time, as I helped Mariella with her *hearing*, I understood my own gift. I knew where to put my hands because I heard a voice in my head. *"Put your hands on her heart... Stay there a little while longer... Go to her ears."* I often heard what I was supposed to do. I had never understood that it was a gift. It seemed so very natural to me that I took it for granted.

I realized that I had always *heard* things: new ideas, voices, dialogues, the beginnings of stories, what I should do next. I also heard observations such as, *"Oh, this person has low self-esteem."* Or, *"She's lonely."* Sometimes the voice came in the form of a suggestion such as, *"Tell her about the lecture. She needs to know about it."* Occasionally I even received directives like, *"You'd better leave or you're going to miss that bus."* I vowed to pay a lot more attention to the voices in my head.

Around this time, I had an experience that highlighted my clair-audience. On a cold, grey winter day, I was taking a walk along the East River, watching my breath turn to steam in the cold air. Suddenly I was overcome with panic that it was my birthday and I had forgotten all about it. My birthday was still a few weeks away. Or was it? I reminded myself that after celebrating it for more than three decades, I knew my birthday.

When I got home, I played back the one message on my answering machine. "Diane," my girlfriend said on the tape recording, "I think it's your birthday. I'm so sorry I forgot. I am in Washington, D.C. today. But I just want to wish you a Happy Birthday."

Another time, I took a vow of silence for a few days during a retreat. At one point during my silent period, I was serving in the bakery. I handed a woman a piece of coconut cake.

"How did you know I wanted that?" She asked.

"You told me," I replied, puzzled by the question. I broke my silence because we were supposed to speak when necessary while offering seva.

"No," she shook her head. "I was thinking I wanted that cake. But I didn't say a word."

I told a friend who was also a student of the Teacher, that I could some-times hear people thinking. "Okay," he said. "What am I thinking?"

I immediately regretted my claim. All of a sudden it sounded to me like boasting, although really I was just trying to make sense of it. I got very quiet and tuned in. "I don't hear anything," I said sheepishly. "I'm just see-ing light."

"Oh, I was just repeating the mantra," he replied. "But that is a form of spiritual light."

I believe people are more telepathic than they know. Our thoughts are like subtle radio waves and we are always transmitting and receiving. Most people just don't realize they are hearing things instead of thinking or imag-ining them. Sometimes I'll think something and the person I'm with will answer me, as if I've spoken aloud.

A Call To Heal

CHAPTER 40

Passing A Test

I SEEMED TO "SLEEP" through many journeys during the Flow Alignment & Connection workshop. Yet by the end, I was directed from within in all my healings. I simply knew or saw or felt or heard what was wrong and what to do to shift it. Who was doing that directing? My own higher Self? Spirit guides? Masters? The other person's higher self? Probably all of the above.

I made several lasting friends, including Judy, a CPA, married to a federal agent. She sometimes joked, "I channel the tax code," because the right book would fall off the shelf and open to just the right page to answer her tax problems. She also ran a large commercial farm in Nebraska. She was able to track energy, especially the energy on business situations and deals. My friend Nancy, a doctor who had a beautiful way of seeing the healing light, was also at the workshop.

On the final day of the course Amy Skezas, the instructor, handed out diplomas to everyone except me. I didn't think it mattered since I'd only gone to the workshop as research for my book. Still, after some hesitation, I spoke up. "Amy, what about my diploma?" It had been left, by error, at her office; she sent an assistant to go pick it up.

"Oh, you had to claim your healership," my friend Thomas said gleefully, when I told him.

That healership was pressed into service immediately. I left the workshop to head to downtown San Francisco, where I had a meeting with Elizabeth Targ, M.D., then a psychiatrist at California Pacific Medical Center, who was heading up a ground-breaking study of long distance healing. I had three hours to get there.

I waited at the bus stop as one bus after another passed me by. The buses only came every half-hour. I now had less than an hour to make my trip. I knew I was going to be late. Finally, I flagged down a passerby who told me that I was at the wrong bus stop.

When I finally caught the bus and stepped inside, the driver asked me, "How is everything going?"

"Terrible," I said, instead of making meaningless small talk. I told him how I had waited in the wrong place for more than an hour. As he drove his route, the bus driver and I began chatting. Soon I had told him I was writing a book on healing. Then he told me his ex-wife had recently been diagnosed with a recurrence of breast cancer and their only child was doing poorly at school. I sensed that his ex-wife was probably going to pass from the cancer. I promised to do a healing. I, in turn, shared with him how I was running late for an important interview.

"When we reach the terminal, stay on the bus," the driver told me. "I'll drive you straight to your appointment. It's my lunch break then." The driver chauffeured me over the Golden Gate Bridge in my own private bus and dropped me off a block from my appointment. I made it to my interview on time.

When I thought about this incident, I felt that I had missed my bus just so this man's ex-wife and child would receive some badly needed healing light.

"That's what happens when you stand up as a healer," Thomas said. He laughed at the ironic perfection, something I couldn't quite yet see.

CHAPTER 41

Time To Write

MY TIME AT *VARIETY* was so magical that I wondered if I would ever sit down and write my book. I enjoyed editing the special sections, punching out articles, and hanging out with my colleagues. It was so much easier than distilling years of interviews and research and writing a book.

There was only one thorn in my side: my direct supervisor. His angry tone chafed at me. For whatever reason, I irritated him as well. Fortunately, he was in Los Angeles and I was in New York. Yet over time, his verbal abuse became harder to ignore.

One day, on the spur of the moment during a walk in the East River Park, I began to recapitulate him. It didn't take long to see the result. As soon as I got home, he rang me. A storm of epic proportions broke out between us over the telephone.

One more time Peter Bart acted as an angel in my life. This time we met at the bar of the Mark Hotel. Peter had a twinkle in his eye as I told him what was going on. I think he found the situation amusing.

"Your book is what is important," he said. "This job is to give you money. You must write your book."

With that, he released me from my contract a few weeks early, noting that I had put in a year's work already. I didn't know it then, but it would be my last job in journalism, so I am glad I enjoyed it as much as I did. It was perfect timing. I needed to do the final research and start writing my book. I had needed a push from the universe and I got it.

CHAPTER 42

Bending Reality

ILL GOUGH, AN enthusiastic and curious scientist then in his sixties, picked up a spoon in the Chinese restaurant in Times Square where we had met for lunch. He twisted the handle in one smooth movement as if it was as malleable as a plastic straw. Then he did it again. When he finished, the metal spoon had two knots in it.

I picked up my spoon and tried to do the same. I couldn't bend it for anything.

"How did you do that?" I asked suspiciously. "Can I see your spoon?"

Bill handed over his spoon. It was the same as mine. "So how did you do it? It's a trick, isn't it?"

"I asked the same thing the first time I saw this," Bill told me. "But I watched my twelve-year-old son bend a spoon."

"Maybe you're just stronger."

"No," he said. "You could bend that spoon if you wanted to."

"How?"

"You just intend it," Bill said. "That softens the molecules of the spoon. Tests show that the molecules literally change their shape in spoon bending."

Bill had spent his career at the Atomic Energy Commission and the

U.S. Department of Energy. More recently he organized the Foundation for Mind-Being Research in Los Altos, California, to investigate subtle energy, consciousness and healing.

I tuned into his energy state and I got it. All I had to do was merge with the spoon, become one with it, just as I would do in a healing. Then we would bend together.

I held my hand on the spoon, meditating on it, while I ran my energy centers. The spoon began to vibrate under my fingers. The metal got hot. I felt a deep oneness with it. When I twisted and knotted it, it bent like butter in my hands.

"Wow," I said, amazed. It was a visceral example to me of the power of resonance and intention, the forces I brought to every healing I did.

To this day, every time I teach spoon bending to my energy students, I think of that afternoon with Bill. He opened a door for me and I open that same door for others. It's a tangible way for people to experience the transformative power of love and intention.

CHAPTER 43

A Physics of Love

ONE DAY, MY friends Thomas, Trudy, and I spent hours together doings healings for each other in Trudy's office. The next day she discovered her printer wasn't working. It produced only a black smear instead of a page of print.

I sensed that the printer had been affected by all of the energy from our healings. I did a long distance healing on the printer to see if I could rebalance it. When I got into a very deep state, to my astonishment I merged with the printer as if it was alive with consciousness. It was extremely intense. Afterwards, the printer worked like new. I had grown somewhat accustomed to my mystical experiences during healings. But merging with a computer printer boggled my mind.

Shortly after this experience, I had my first meeting with Robert Jahn, Ph.D, the dean emeritus of the Princeton School of Engineering and Applied Science. At the time, Jahn directed one of the most extraordinary physics research projects in the world, studying the influence of consciousness on physical reality: mind over matter.

After we had talked awhile, I screwed up the courage to tell him about my healing experience with the printer. I was curious to hear what he would think. "Congratulations," he said to my surprise. He asserted that I had used a perfectly normal human ability. Something in my soul settled then and there: This brilliant scientist, who had worked for NASA, knew what I was talking about.

From the moment I had first stumbled on energy healing, I believed that if energy healing was real, then there had to be a scientific explanation. Even though healing is a deeply spiritual experience, I just couldn't accept the phenomena would be outside of natural laws.

I poured over scientific journals and was surprised to find how much research had been done, including double blind studies. I learned many things that eventually influenced the way I worked as a healer. Nevertheless, when I first came across the research from the PEAR Lab, I was stunned. I was looking at nearly two decades of pure research that described the very experiences of healers.

That's when I became convinced that healing was future medicine. One era's mystical domain is another's scientific frontier. Just think of the heavens in the time of Galileo. I believe that one day, people will look back and shake their heads in wonderment at what we didn't know about subtle energy. They will consider these the dark ages.

The Princeton lab was run by Dr. Jahn and his lab manager and research partner, psychologist Brenda Dunne. They used random number generators in their research. The principle was similar to studying coin flips. Could people influence the outcome of a series of coin flips to get more heads or tails, simply by setting an intention to do so? The question proposed in the Princeton lab, however, was whether people could influence — by intention alone — a random number generator on a computer. If the computer was randomly spewing out numbers above and below 100, could a person set their intent to see more numbers over 100 and get that result? Could a person set an intention to see more numbers below 100, say 99.78988, and see the computer produce that result? Could a person, simply by intention influence the results of the computer?

They did millions of computer runs with hundreds of different volunteer operators coming into the lab to sit with the computers and set an intention. When they looked at the results, the PEAR Lab found that people did subtly affect the numbers generated simply by intent. It took thousands of trials to see the effects, but the probability that they were chance occurrences was one in a billion. People even influenced the base line. The numbers were too perfectly close to 100.00 in experiments designed to set a baseline to be random.

Dr. Jahn and Dunne also found that each person has a unique influence on reality, a kind of signature, in the same way that you can tell that a painting is by a particular artist.

This signature style is something we see everywhere in life. For instance, have you ever noticed that some people always have trouble with their computers and printers? And other people can have one computer after another that never gives them a problem? Or have you seen how one person is a magnet for car accidents while another person never has an accident?

We all have a subtle influence on reality. And it produces a signature style. We will have the same type of experiences again and again. From the point of view of Jahn and Dunne's research, this isn't just chance, but a manifestation of some aspect of our consciousness.

Dr. Jahn and Dunne also found that a pair of operators has their own unique signature style. If you teamed up Mr. A and Miss B, you would get a pattern that was unique to the pair. It was not the sum of their individual styles, however. It was its own unique consciousness. If you then paired up Mr. A and Miss D, you'd get another unique signature style.

In addition, the studies showed that the influence people could have on the random number generators transcend time. People could affect the random number generator before the machine was turned on or, even, after it was turned off. Indeed, the result would be the same as when they set their intent while the machine was on.

Likewise, distance didn't seem to exist. If an operator ran a test from Paris while the computer was in Princeton, New Jersey, the result would be the same as if the operator was sitting in Princeton in a room with the machine.

Ultimately, Dr. Jahn and Dunne found that the most successful test results came from people who experienced a sense of "resonance" or union. These people literally talked about experiencing a bond with the machine, of "falling in love" or "merging" or "having fun" with it just as I had done with the printer, and as I did with people in every healing. The driving force of the universe, according to Dr. Jahn: "It's Love. Love with a capital "L."

For Dr. Jahn, love isn't just a mystical experience. It's one of the foundations of physics, the force that moves everything in the universe, including quantum particles.

This research stunned and soothed me. It described pretty much every experience I'd ever had as a healer. The research was such a confirmation of the extraordinary reality that I had entered. Sometimes it took my breath away.

Eventually, I became friends with Jahn and Dunne and the other scientists working at the lab. Once, I did a spoon bending demonstration for everyone in the lab. I used the spoons they kept for mixing teas and other hot beverages. The next time I came to the lab, I noticed the spoons I had knotted were still part of the lab's silverware collection, resting in a mug as if they were normal spoons.

CHAPTER 44

Inner Vision

EVEN AS I was wrapping up my reporting, I found myself attending several of Rosalyn Bruyere's workshops. I was still trying to get all the details I needed. However, what I gained above all was more of an understanding of myself. Being around Bruyere was a balm for my third eye. She was stunningly clairvoyant. Being in her field gave me the permission I needed in order to *see*. It happened simply by resonance, as if I was keenly attuned to her energy field. She never instructed me or debriefed me. *Seeing* just happened for me in her presence.

Once, at a retreat workshop, Rosalyn's students were gathered around her in a semi-circle. One by one, they handed her their favorite healing tools: precious stones, shamanic rattles, and beautiful multi-faceted crystals.

Rosalyn lovingly took each item and held it in her hand. As she did, I saw a stream of energy running from her into the object, and then back into Rosalyn. I could hardly believe it. She was communicating with these objects, asking them questions and receiving answers. They appeared to be conscious. When the circuit was completed, she relayed to the owner of the object what it had told her of its true power and purpose.

I looked around, wondering if anyone else saw what I saw. I couldn't tell. I realized it didn't matter. I had *seen* it. It was real.

MY INNER VISION was starting to click at the most unexpected moments, even when I wasn't trying to see anything. Once at a dinner party, I leaned back and rlaxed with a glass of water in hand and suddenly saw a flow of energy like a river, going out from all the doctors at the table towards a particularly prominent physician. They were literally giving their power away. But this wasn't unprompted. The famous physician was subtly demanding their fealty. None of them were conscious of what they were doing. They would have been horrified.

At another dinner party, as I looked at a guest sitting at the far end of the table, his body dissolved into fields of energy, as if in a Cubist painting. Physically, this man looked rigid. Yet his energy was even more rigid. How painful that must be, I thought to myself.

When he shifted in his chair, I turned away, embarrassed that I had been staring. At that moment, I realized he hadn't consciously noticed my gaze at all. The vision had occurred outside of space-time, in what would be a nano-second of ordinary time.

I never knew when or where this type of seeing would occur. But I found that with each layer of healing I did for myself, my seeing expanded. When I laid hands on people, seeing and knowing was always there.

CHAPTER 45

The Healing Touch

M OST HEALING WORKSHOPS are designed to let students work on each other. Typically people in these groups are relatively healthy. But at a practicum for advanced students, Rosalyn Bruyere invited about a dozen very seriously ill people to receive healings.

At first, I accompanied Rosalyn around the room. We were just getting started when I glanced across the room and saw flames shooting out of one woman's abdomen. They seemed so vivid, it was a little frightening.

"That woman has flames coming out of her abdomen," I said excitedly to Rosalyn. Rosalyn looked at where I was pointing. "Yes, she does."

"What does that mean?" I asked.

"We'll have to see," Bruyere replied. When we approached the patient, Bruyere confirmed my sense that there was an inflammation in the woman's gut and a lot of anger.

Next Rosalyn stopped at the table where students were treating a man with a degenerative neurological disorder. Rosalyn put her hands on the patient's feet and began to run energy up his legs. "You're running gold," I exclaimed. I didn't see the color gold. But I felt it. And I knew it.

"Yes," she said.

"A lucky guess," I said.

Rosalyn turned to me. "Don't ever discredit your vision," she said quietly, still running gold light into the man on the table.

Eventually, Rosalyn asked me to join one of the teams of healers. Soon a woman who was in an advanced stage of metastasized breast cancer was sent to our group. She was in her 40s, but so fragile she needed a walker to support herself. In a voice that was barely above a whisper, she told us the cancer had taken up residence in her bones; she was in constant pain. She didn't have the strength to get on the table so we worked with her as she sat in a chair.

I could see this woman was suffering. Yet nothing prepared me for what happened when I laid my hands on her. I could feel the cancer running up and down her bones like mice scampering in the floorboards. Her bones were screaming in pain, but the rest of her body was deadly silent, as if most of her essence had already left. Laying hands on her, I merged with her, her pain, and her cancer. We became one.

Five healers held the same "red" energy of vitality. Another five healers held a focus of energy and healing intent around us. The woman got a tremendous blast of life force. My understanding of cancer was forever transformed. Laying hands on her, I had a much more intimate understanding of her suffering, and the suffering of so many others, than I had ever had before. I was inside her. There was nothing intellectual or distant about the connection. We were one.

Four days later, this same woman walked in for her next treatment without her walker and wearing lipstick. The healings certainly hadn't cured her, but subtle energy had given her something that powerful painkillers, chemotherapy and radiation had not—vitality, and an ability to take some small pleasure in being alive. We were overjoyed for her.

After that, I couldn't do enough healings.

CHAPTER 46

God's Healing Clinic

I ENTERED A NEW phase where I ran into people who, metaphorically speaking, wore a sign saying: "Please Heal."

Elaine was a beautician. I found her while looking in the yellow pages for someone who could do eyebrow shaping. Her name lit up.

The first thing I noticed when she opened the door to her apartment was the sour odor emanating from the kitchen. It turned out that Elaine suffered from a chronic, systemic yeast infection and was always cooking up something to help herself.

After a few visits, I offered to do a healing. She readily accepted. As I connected soul-to-soul, I could feel her loneliness and low self-esteem. I added light to shift and uplift her.

I had barely gone a half-block after leaving Elaine when I became possessed by an overwhelming desire to eat cake. I felt as if I had a demon inside. I had to dig my heels into the sidewalk so that I wouldn't be swept into the bakery on the corner. Realizing the ravenous, insatiable hunger was Elaine's, the desire dissolved. I was myself again.

"Do you like to eat cake?" I asked Elaine the next time I saw her.

"Oh yes," she said with great enthusiasm. "Sometimes I'll just stuff it in my mouth. I crave it. And it's exactly the worst thing for me to eat. It feeds the yeast infection. But I can't help myself," She paused. "Why do you ask?"

"Just curious," I replied.

The second healing was no easier. As I began to run energy, a wave of nausea hit me so hard I could hardly stand. Elaine could never have adequately described to me the intensity of her cravings, or the agony of her nausea. But I felt it viscerally. "Do you ever get nauseous?" I gently asked.

"Yes," Elaine replied. "Whenever I eat cake or drink coffee."

I transmuted the nausea during the second healing. After just these two sessions, Elaine started a new diet and, for the first time, was able to stay on it. She no longer had the kind of cravings that had driven her, and she no longer felt nauseous most of the day.

MY EXPERIENCE WITH Elaine was just the beginning. On my way to a meditation at the Self Realization Fellowship center in Manhattan I found myself again being invited to offer healing light. On this particular evening, as I approached the meditation center, I saw a group of people milling about. This was highly unusual. Everyone was always inside when I got there. I scanned the crowd for Thomas, who I always met there, but he was not in the group. Instead as I reached the crowd, a tall, thin, blond man approached me. I had never seen him at the meditations. I knew immediately that he had AIDS.

"What's going on?" I asked.

"We're locked out. The person with the key hasn't arrived. He's already a half-hour late."

The tall man looked at me, first as a stranger, then with a sense of recognition. At almost the same moment, I, too, realized that I somehow knew him.

"Did you go on a teen bike trip?" he asked. "To the Canadian Rockies?"

"Yes," I replied, shocked.

"Diane, It's Jon," he said, extending his hand. My hand was already out to his. "Jon," I said. "My God."

We had bicycled together through the Canadian Rockies as teens. The trip was so arduous that it was my first and last long bicycle trek. But I had always felt fondly towards Jon and we had remained in touch afterwards.

When the building was still locked fifteen minutes later, Jon and I went to a local coffee shop. Over hot drinks, Jon told me that he had

AIDS. "You're so lucky," he said after bringing me up to date on his medical situation and his life, and I shared a little bit about my journey. "To have all these experiences, to do healing work, to see that side of life. I wish I had some sense of the spirit." He burst into tears.

"Jon," I said, "You can have that, too."

I invited Jon back to my place for a healing. "Oh, Mother Meera," he exclaimed when we entered my apartment, looking at a picture of her. "She says you can write her and she will always answer. But I wrote her and she never answered me," he said sadly. "I never got a letter."

"I'm sure she answered you. It's not always in the form of a letter," I explained. "It's an answer inside. That's how she would answer me."

I invited Jon to lie down on my couch. As soon as I placed my hands on Jon, I felt this immensely loving presence envelope me, as if Mother Meera's light had entered me. Perhaps Jon received the answer to his letter right then and there, with me serving as the conduit.

As I transmitted energy, I found that Jon had a deep schism between his solar plexus and his heart, and a rift between his left and right side. I worked on healing the split and holding grace so he would know that he was always safe and loved.

When I got to know Jon better, I realized what a remarkable spiritual experience he was having. Although he had few T-cells Jon rarely got sick, even with a cold. He meditated every day. After taking anti-viral medicine for a few months, he had thrown them away, and he lived for many years without them before turning to them again. I am sure it was his spiritual practices that kept Jon so healthy.

CHAPTER 47

Guided From Within

W ITH EACH HEALING I learned more about the power of the energy.

When I did a healing, I often touched the origin of a person's suffering and helped to dissolve it. Even when I touched pain, as I so often did, there was the bliss of union, the bliss of the Divine Light.

The understanding I received when laying hands on people was something no conversation or textbook could ever have imparted to me. For instance, when I first worked on someone with chronic fatigue I couldn't believe how exhausted and lethargic they felt. Every time I have laid hands on someone with this condition since then, I have been overcome with the tiredness with which the person is struggling.

I also discovered the energy state for high blood pressure by experiencing it. As I ran energy for a friend, I came in contact with an intense pressure in his field. I had never before worked with someone who had high blood pressure, but I knew that's what I was touching.

Many times, I asked the Teacher for the wisdom and grace to understand karma and energy patterning. Originally, I wanted to alleviate my own suffering; now I wanted to be of service to others.

As I did healings, I was able to see how the subtle thoughts, feelings and beliefs shape people's bodies and experiences. It is a multi-dimensional influence that spans time and space.

Once I did a healing for a woman who had been a radio announcer, before her vocal chords had been paralyzed. Now she could barely speak above a rasping whisper. As I ran energy I had the sense that she had misused the power of the word and had prevented others from speaking up. It was so vivid that I gently mentioned it. She nodded emphatically; she already knew.

Karma isn't a punishment. It's more like a law of physics, where action can create an equal and opposite reaction. One way or another, we experience the fruits of our actions—both good and not so good. Sometimes I wish more people knew that there are consequences for their actions; it might save them from doing ill to others and then suffering later on.

As I worked with others, I discovered that my meditation practice was essential to developing my skill as a healer. It cleared my psyche so I was free to help another person clear their issues. Meditation also taught me to quiet my mind. Then, during a healing, in the union of soul energies, I shared the same psyche, the same heart with the person receiving the healing light. When my mind was still, it was like having a laser beam of psychic force. I could bring total focus and coherence to bear on the problem of another.

CHAPTER 48

Surrender

A FTER FIVE YEARS of reporting and writing, *Infinite Grace* was finally published in June 1999. (It was reissued as *How People Heal* in paperback.) I couldn't wait to get a new job on a magazine. My bank account had dwindled terribly. My psyche wasn't in much better shape.

Have you ever heard the saying: How do you make God laugh? Tell him your plans. Well, God was laughing. There I was writing letters to different magazines, sending my clips and my resume. In the meantime, I gave talks at bookstores and healing centers and did radio and television interviews. Wherever I went people always asked me for healings. This seemed odd to me, and generally I turned them down. In my mind, I was a journalist. I never once said I was a healer.

But I longed to help people. Soon after my book came out, I was invited to give a talk at Canyon Ranch in Tucson, Arizona. When I arrived at the spa, I noticed one particular woman who, I sensed, was very sad and in need of help. I wanted to rush right over to her and lay hands on her. But I knew it wasn't appropriate. Later, at dinner, a spunky older woman told me that she was going blind.

Both women showed up at my evening talk. When I offered to do a healing demonstration, the two women were the first to volunteer to receive healings. First I did a healing for the woman who was going blind. I saw that she was in denial about her fear of blindness. I held light for her to come to terms with her situation. Then I did a healing for the woman who seemed so sad. It turned out her mother had recently committed suicide because she was going blind. She had been losing her sight to the same disease that the first woman was facing. I could never make up a synchronicity like this. The juxtaposition of these two healings underscored the seriousness of the first woman's situation.

After these sessions, several guests called me in my room asking if they could have a healing. I told them I was a journalist and encouraged them to find a healer.

The next night, I participated in a panel on healing and mediumship. One of the other participants was the medium Laurie Campbell. There was an immediate, deep bond as if we had known each other for a long time.

Laurie and I indeed became friends. I did healings for her dad in the last few years of his life. She conveyed some important messages to me and I will always be grateful to her. She told me a few months after we met, while I was imagining *Infinite Grace* landing on the bestseller list, that not much was going to happen with that book for years. I was more than a little upset. It turned out she was totally right.

Ultimately her warning, which took a lot of courage to deliver, helped me to accept that it was all turning out as it was supposed to be. (Now, of course, I'm grateful the book's publication unfolded as it did. God is much smarter than I am.)

Later that year, Laurie gave me a set of luggage for Christmas. Again, as much as I loved Laurie, I thought she was tuning into the wrong frequency. For one thing, I had cleaned out all of my clutter and I didn't want to start collecting new clutter. The luggage was just going to sit in my closet, collecting dust or end up under my bed, which would be even worse for the feng shui.

She insisted I take the luggage. "You are going to need it," she predicted. "You are going to be traveling a lot." Well, the luggage did sit in my closet for almost two years. But after that, I used it so much I wore it out.

That weekend at Canyon Ranch I also had an immediate resonance with the Reverend Anne Gehman, a spiritualist minister, who runs the Church for Spiritual Truth in Falls Church, Virginia. Rev. Gehman is a grande dame of the Spiritualist world. While I still lived in New

York, Rev. Gehman graciously invited me to speak at her church several times, and to teach workshops on healing to interested members of the congregation.

My world was moving further and further from journalism. Yet, I still had a very fixed idea about who I was. I went to my first job interview with great excitement. We hadn't been chatting long when the editor opened up about a lot of challenges she'd been having. Before I knew it, she was crying. Something in my energy field seemed to set an automatic healing space. I was happy to talk to her and help her. But I knew I wouldn't be getting the job.

The very same thing happened on my next interview with an editor at a different publication. That's when I knew, maybe things weren't going my way for a journalism job. It still took months before I could accept that I was banging on a door that had been slammed shut. I couldn't get it to budge, even a little bit.

Finally I saw that everything that was happening—the lack of job offers, the constant requests for healings—was guidance. I remembered what Rosalyn Bruyere once told me in a workshop when I asked a question about a vision I had: "You have certain gifts you must develop and use." Even the Teacher had once addressed my purpose. "Medicine?" she asked me during a meeting. "No. I'm a writer," I replied, puzzled.

I went to my first healer, Dianne, for a session to receive guidance. She led me in a shamanic journey in which I ended up swimming in a beautiful stream. The most radiant sunlight poured over me, dappling the water, the trees and the rocks. "Everything is going to be okay," she said. "It's your destiny to be a healer."

CHAPTER 49

A Magic Carpet

FROM THE BEGINNING, I loved offering healing light to people. It is always blissful to connect heart to heart. But I soon learned how much suffering is hidden just below the surface. Even at a dinner party, you will tap into this truth if you take the time to genuinely talk to people. The great thing is being able to help alleviate some of that suffering.

I saw all of this clearly from the start. Early on, I did a workshop for a group of WBAI Radio listeners as part of a fundraising for the New York station. When I connected with each person, I found that everyone there had something they were dealing with. One woman, who looked healthy at first glance, had brain cancer.

People often ask me if a healer takes on the karma of the other person, and the answer is no—at least that's not the wisest way to do things. But a healer does feel what is going on in the other person and sometimes it can be intense. I experience those vibrations not only in the other person, but in my own being as well. That's how I know what someone is feeling.

If a healer works with a person who has an issue where the healer has a sensitivity—watch out! I learned this through experience, the way I seemed to learn everything.

A gentleman volunteered to receive a healing at an evening workshop. His presenting issue was advanced lung cancer. Then he mentioned that he had been a heavy alcoholic as a younger man, although he had been dry for twenty years. I have always been super sensitive to alcohol and I'd never been a drinker. Even a glass of wine could give me a headache that lasts for days. That night, I was in a fragile state anyway. I knew I was in for it. When I laid hands on this gentleman, I could feel and taste the alcohol. The energy of it was still in his field and was now being drained away.

When I finished the healing, I had to excuse myself and go throw up. It was as if I had had too much to drink. That night, I prayed and meditated for hours. In the early morning, I woke to find that I was still incredibly sick. Praying for help, I fell back to sleep. An hour later, I came to consciousness feeling whole and refreshed. I happened to mention the experience later that day to my friend Laurie Campbell. She said she'd had a dream that morning where I was calling for help. She gave me healing light.

That is the only time I've had that reaction to someone's former alcohol addiction. I learned a lesson then. When I do healings for people who have just come out of major surgery, I am careful to monitor what is going on. I feel everything the patient has experienced, and have to clear their energy of the anesthesia, drugs and trauma. Sometimes it is so intense that I have to pause and re-balance myself before I can continue. But as I do the healing, all of that heavy energy gets released, speeding the person's physical healing. It can make a dramatic difference to have a healing directly before and/or after surgery.

Everything I learned in my own healing journey became part of my tool kit as I ministered to others. For instance, I offered the Recapitulation to certain men and women who had ongoing difficulties in their relationships. I even encouraged a woman to recapitulate a business partner who had ill intent. Within weeks, the difficult partner dissolved out of the business.

As a healer, I am a conduit, a servant of the light. The outcome of a healing doesn't belong to me. There are many factors that influence a healing— the intention of the person receiving the healing, the depth of the issue, and many soul factors—that we can't always know.

Sometimes, I don't even learn the outcome of the healing. Once, for instance, in the very early days of my practice, I did a session with a guitarist suffering from carpal tunnel syndrome. I only learned five years later, when she sent a friend to me, that the guitarist attributed that one healing with saving her music career.

Another early experience showed me just how much surrender and faith in God's plan I would need to offer light to others. Evangelina, a beautiful woman in her thirties, had a cancer that was wrapped around her optic nerve, requiring surgery. She had already lost the vision in one eye as an infant when it became cancerous. She was understandably desperate to save the sight in her remaining eye. So when doctors performed the surgery, she told them to spare the nerve, even if it meant leaving some cancer behind.

She found her way to me after the surgery, when she was taking chemotherapy. She had very little vision, perhaps able to see some shadows and light. In one of our sessions, determined to break the pattern, I repeated mantras for Lord Ganesh, the Hindu deity with the power to remove obstacles, hoping to invoke his energy. To me it seemed if ever there was an obstacle, this cancer qualified.

Much to my surprise, Ganesh literally appeared on the inner planes in my healing room. He looked just as he is always depicted, with a human body and the head of an elephant. As I watched, I saw him use his trunk to suck the cancer out from around her optic nerve.

Soon after, Evangelina had a new cat scan. It showed all signs of the tumor gone. Often, there is a watery mark around a site where cancer has been. But even this was gone. This was remarkable news, since doctors had given her a poor prognosis in regards to beating the cancer. The doctor said Evangelina's vision should return within a few months. But although her optic nerve looked fine, at least in the six months to a year in which I heard reports, her vision did not recover. Healing is always a mysterious process. In Evangelina's case the physical was only one level that needed healing.

Each healing I did opened up a mystical world. Whatever the outcome, I was allowed to connect soul to soul and offer light. The psychic Laurie Campbell had told me that the process of researching, writing and publishing *Infinite Grace* was "a magic carpet." I eventually came to see that she was right. The book transported me to a new life.

CHAPTER 50

The Divine Heart

O VER THE CHRISTMAS holidays in 1999, I flew to California to be with the Teacher on retreat. At first I was terrified. "It's the shakti, the energy," my companion behind the bakery counter at the retreat said reassuringly. "It's going to be okay." After she said that, I knew that she was right. I calmed down.

The retreat began even before I left home. In the weeks leading up to it, I found myself repeating Sanskrit mantras in my dreams. These were mantras I had never heard in my waking life. Later, at the retreat, I learned from the Teacher that she had been working with us on the subtle planes, repeating these mantras with us.

While I experienced those sessions as dreams, I realized they were real meetings, happening in a higher dimension. My soul body was called by the Teacher to these events.

Even getting to California involved a testing of my soul. A fierce snowstorm in Chicago, where I had a connecting flight, kept my plane grounded on the runway at La Guardia airport in New York City. As precious time passed, I was in increasing danger of missing my connection and, as a result, the intensive meditation program. All of a sudden, I realized the outcome wasn't up to me. I became intoxicatingly calm, almost blissful. Just then the pilot finally began taxiing us back to the gate.

Back at the terminal, I ran to the gate for a connecting plane that would take me through sunny Dallas instead of Chicago. By then it was my only chance of getting to California that day. The plane was still there! I couldn't believe my good fortune. Then an airline attendant stopped me. "Where are you going?" she said.

"I'm trying to make the plane to Dallas," I said, pointing to the jet.

"It already departed," she said. "That's a different plane."

I must have looked stricken.

"Where are you going?" she asked. "Maybe I can help you?"

I told her that I was scheduled to fly into Long Beach but my destination was a nearby city. She looked at the computer and found a route through Dallas, directly to where I needed to be. I had tried to get that flight originally months ago, but it had been booked.

"The flight is overbooked," the attendant said a moment later. My heart sank. She paused for a minute, looking at her screen intently. "I'm going to put you on the flight anyway," she said. I was so grateful. It seemed like a miracle.

When I got to Dallas, I discovered that my connecting my flight to California was indeed overbooked. The airline paid some passengers to get off and take a later plane. But I made it to the weekend course.

At the retreat, I had a room only for the first night. I had planned to stay with a friend for the first week. But the car that I had planned to borrow broke down a few days before I left New York. Now I would have to stay at the retreat. But when I called around, I learned that all the hotels were booked.

As I stood in the lobby of the retreat center that first day, a woman whom I liked very much, but knew only casually, called my name. We embraced happily.

"My gosh," she said when I told her about my situation. "Come stay with me." She mentioned one of the most luxurious hotels in the area. "My mother had to cancel. I have an extra queen bed in the room." I moved in the next night. I took the weekend program as planned and had another luxurious ten days of retreat to unfold before me.

CHRISTMAS DAY BEGAN with a meditation program. I wore my white and gold sari, the one I had worn in my very first dream with the Teacher, when I had waved the sacred lights of the Arati to her. When the Teacher came into the room, she walked down the aisle where

I was standing. As her eyes fell on me, she paused for an instant. I could almost hear her thinking, "Oh, there you are."

Later that day, as I finished lunch, a sudden, intense silence descended on the café. I had eaten alone at a table full of strangers and had been feeling sorry for myself. Now my mood lifted. I knew instinctively that the Teacher had entered the room.

Slowly and deliberately, she walked through the café. Once again, she turned down the aisle where I stood. This time she stopped before the woman in front of me.

"So this is where you are hiding your husband," the Teacher said to this woman. As she spoke, she turned her gaze to me and settled on my heart. I didn't know what message she was trying to convey. Was it something about the husband that I could never find? If so, what?

The Teacher moved on. When she had passed out of sight, I bused my tray and headed to the bakery to offer my time. I had barely stepped behind the counter when I noticed that the mantra was repeating itself in my heart. It was rhythmic, intense and absorbing and growing stronger. I felt flushed and dizzy and could barely stand up. I found I had no control over it and couldn't stop or change it, even if I wanted to.

As quickly as I could, I went to my room to lie down. I didn't know anything, except bliss. I remained absorbed in this divine pulsation for the rest of the day and night. I couldn't get up for dinner, nor did I have any desire for food or company. I was awash in waves of love.

I had come so far. Little did I know then that I was just at the beginning of a great journey.

Epilogue

ALMOST TWO DECADES have passed since my spiritual initiation. I've had many further experiences on the inner planes, which I hope to share in the future. Thanks to the light, I have grown more and more steady. Many of my dreams, which seemed so impossible, have come true.

I continue to serve as a healer and am very grateful to offer light to others. It is as fulfilling and fascinating and mysterious as the day I started. I see people in my offices in Santa Monica and New York. I also do long distance healings with people around the world—connecting to people as far away (or as close) as Europe, Australia and Japan.

I now live in California with my husband, a sweet, perceptive and funny man. It is a first marriage for both of us and by the time we met, we had been looking for each other for many years. We are both quiet people, and well-suited to each other. Recently we were blessed with a son.

Although I have been teaching energy skills and healing since *Infinite Grace* was first published, I am still a student of the energy and always will be. I meditate and pray daily and do many other spiritual practices. The Teacher is still teaching me and for that I am grateful beyond words.

So much has changed on the inside that I am a different person than the one who began to investigate healing so many years ago.

I am very grateful to travel in the company of the light.

Acknowledgements

I'D LIKE TO thank the healers who have been both mentors and friends, including Rosalyn Bruyere, Gerda Swearengen, Thomas Carl Ayers, Dianne Arnold, Amy Skezas and all others in my "Psychic Friends Network," including Julie Hoyle, Laurie Campbell, Nancy Reuben, Judy Eggleston, Calixte Stamp, Alice Gregory, Catherine Karas, Christopher Stewart, Lorrie Kazan and Allison DuBois.

I also want to thank everyone who assisted me in getting this book out to the world. A special thanks to Michael A. Gerber for his excellent editorial guidance; Randall Leers for his brilliant design, light and intuition; and to Karen Campbell, Linda Beugg and Susan Kim Flanagan for input on design, title and publishing process.

I also want to thank everyone with whom I have worked with as a healer. I have learned something about the divine nature of existence from each of you. Thank you and blessings always.

Many thanks to the scientists studying consciousness, especially Brenda Dunne and Robert Jahn. Your work adds so much light.

I'd also like to acknowledge Lars and JoAnn Svanberg for unwavering friendship and hospitality; Sonam Kushner, Jolie Parcher, Susan McArdle and Leslie Handley-White for friendship and for creating the space for me to offer healings in Manhattan and the Hamptons; and to my parents, Roslyn and Howard Goldner, who have always been loving and supportive as I made my way through life.

A special thanks goes to my husband, Michael Randleman, who is always there for me both professionally and personally with the great gifts of love, wisdom and kindness.

My deep gratitude to all the saints and to Mother Meera, and to The Teacher for infinite grace and guidance.

I'd also like to thank you, Dear Reader, for taking the time to read this book and share with me a few moments of the journey to the light.

About Diane

HEALER AND MEDICAL intuitive Diane Goldner helps people facing illness, life and relationship challenges, and those seeking emotional balance. She works with adults, children and infants in Los Angeles and New York, and does long distance healing with people around the country and internationally. She also teaches healing and advanced energy skills to healers, therapists, scientists and many others.

She has discussed healing on dozens of radio and television programs, including on CNN International and Dr. Christiane Northrup's show, "Flourish!" on Hay House Radio, and has given talks at Canyon Ranch, University of Arizona Medical School, Children's Memorial Hospital in Chicago and many other healing centers and book stores.

A former journalist, Diane has written for *The New York Times*, *The Wall Street Journal* and many other publications, and served as a contributing editor for *USA Weekend, Variety* and *Body and Soul*. She has also written about healing for beliefnet.com.

Her first book, *How People Heal*, was originally published in hardcover as *Infinite Grace: Where the Worlds of Science and Spiritual Healing Meet*.

For more information or to sign up for her monthly e-newsletter, workshops or tele-classes go to www.DianeGoldner.com. You can also visit Diane at www.TheFertilityHealer.com or email Diane to set up a healing at dianegoldner@gmail.com.